A
FULFILLED
LEGACY

How To Overcome Money Lies,
And Have Financial Freedom

SANDRA KAIMA

A
FULFILLED
LEGACY

How To Overcome Money Lies,
And Have Financial Freedom

SANDRA KAIMA

Breakfree Forever Publishing

DEDICATION

To my wonderful children Robyn Kaima-Batchelor, Cordelia-Jones Seruwu-Kaima and generations to come. To the readers of this book, I wish that on your way to success, you spread the word to help others find their key to financial empowerment.

ACKNOWLEDGMENTS

My parents, Ham and Betty Kaima have supported me in making my vision a reality.

Barrie Mohamed has motivated and encouraged me to write this book and allowed my purpose to shine.

My sisters have listened to my stories and let me be me - together we rise as one.

Yvette Samuel - Thank you for your encouragement and words of wisdom.

Michelle Watson has reminded me of what my purpose is in life.

Damaris Albaran has been supportive and instrumental in my life, I thank you.

Regina Edwards, who always pushed for my success, may your soul rest in heavenly peace.

Patrice Washington, thank you for your permission to use material from your coaching programmes.

66 *When you can see what is possible and believe that it can come to pass, it makes you capable of doing the impossible.*

Dr Myles Munroe
— The Principles and Power of Vision [1]

---

1 Munroe, Dr. Myles, (2003) *The Principles and Power of Vision; Keys to achieving Personal and Corporate Destiny*, Witticker House, Nassu, Bahamas, p. 18

TABLE OF CONTENTS

INTRODUCTION

This book stems from my Financial Empowerment Programme.[2] It covers the six principles:

1. Empower in earning
2. Empower in spending
3. Empower in overcoming money blocks
4. Empower in savings
5. Empower in investments
6. Empower in giving

Our main goal as individuals is to love ourselves, receive love, and give love. It is not about stressing over tangible things like money.

I am writing this book to empower individuals who want to gain power and control over their finances and live in abundance.

This book is also for you if you feel you're often overlooked or underestimated because you do not fit into the status quo.

This book is for you if you were taught to be 'grateful' for being given opportunities. The truth is that you deserve those opportunities because you have worked hard for them. There is absolutely no requirement for you to lower your expectations. It's okay to want more and reach for the stars.

We must understand that statistics do not determine what is possible for you, both now and in the future. You determine your future by your decisions and actions. You choose how to behave in all circumstances. Whether you say yes or no, you hold the answers as to how far you are willing to go in life. The path is not supposed to be easy. However, with the right guidance, it can be manageable.

We all know that with hard work and absolute determination, you can make your vision a reality. This can happen regardless of your status: single; married; divorced; disabled, etc. I believe our vision comes from God, who will not give us visions to carry out without equipping us with the necessary resources to bring that vision to fruition.

Whatever your faith or belief, you have been given the right vision for you and the equipment to carry out that vision. In my coaching programme, I can help you to bring that vision to life.

Before working on your vision of financial independence, we must believe we can do it. This belief means that we must be open to learning, being coached, and stepping into the limelight.

Far too many of us have had our light dimmed in many ways by prejudices and pure ignorance from others. I want this book to brighten the light for you. I want you to recognise that you can earn extra money and aim to become a millionaire and beyond if that is your desire. If you are cognitively impaired, it can be difficult, but even so, I believe that your caregivers should read this book to be equipped to support you in reaching your true potential, as well as their own.

You see, broken legacies can be restored, if you realise the potential you have stored within you and are willing to do the work to heal any open wounds.

In this book, you will discover that the broken legacies are the lies you tell yourself repeatedly, and by continuing to hold on to those lies, you are choosing to live in the lies. Stepping into the truth means you have to say "I can, I am able, and I will do the necessary work for me to become financially literate and financially equipped to gain financial independence. If not for me but for the sake of my family, community and others."

I hope this book helps you eliminate the financial lies that are holding you back from defining financial success for yourself.

Even with the ongoing challenges you are facing daily and other economic, political, and global issues, you are still in control of your legacy.

The legacy is created by you and rebuilt only from your actions. If you follow the six principles in this book, I know that you will be on your way to mending a fulfilled legacy.

The statistics you read or hear are not wrong to a certain degree; however, they do not and should not determine your reality. They do not know your capability, and only you know what you can do. When people say: *"The doctor said I am not well; therefore, I cannot work,"* it is like you are saying that the doctor knows what you are capable of doing. In reality, they can only diagnose you, give you support for your pain, and possibly give you medication for that health condition. However, they cannot tell you what you can do and cannot determine your capabilities.

I remember when I was pregnant, I kept going to the GP for months. He turned around and said: "*You have been living with this pregnancy for months. You need to tell me what I can do to help you because you know what you need.*"

He gave me the confidence to delve deeper so that I could clearly state what I thought I could do, for example, to go to work but work fewer hours. I had no strength to work the entire day because I had hyperemesis gravidarum.

I was given a sick note reflecting what I knew I could do; this liberated me. I want you to do the same. Ask yourself if you can accomplish your vision. Do the work regardless of your circumstances or what others are saying and doing.

Sometimes the blind man is more determined to see the truth than the one that has been given eyes. The deaf hears nothing negative and, therefore, can only operate in what they believe. I believe it sometimes pays to ignore the noise because this allows you to get on with your life.

One late evening, after I had finished painting my home, I bumped into a friend of a friend on my way to Tesco. He asked me what I was doing up so late at night and I told him I had just finished painting my house and needed a snack. He then asked whether I had a 'sugar daddy' somewhere who was feeding me with cash that allowed me to buy this property that I was now painting. I laughed at his rude suggestion and kindly told him that no rich man in my life had helped me. He was trying to insult my intelligence instead of praising my efforts.

He could see and hear what I was saying but wanted to believe that women could not buy homes unless men were attached to them.

I don't blame him for having this mindset if all he hears on the news or reads in the papers is how poor single parents are and how some women are 'gold diggers.' Tunes like *Gold Digger* by Kanye West only reinforce these beliefs.

I can now see that my friend was stuck in his situation, broke, unemployed and without assets, because of the noise he chose to hear. It helped him justify why he could not do the work. Even if I told him otherwise, his mind was set; it soothed his ego and made him feel better about himself. He had created his own prison and was unwilling to use the keys provided to him to free himself.

66 *If we are unwilling to change our mindset and not willing to look outside our cycle of comfort, then what hope do we have?*

You may want a nice car, a fancy house, or five-star holidays, but you are unwilling to work or seek support to change your situation. As a result, you end up living in jealousy, regret, envy, depression, anxiety, and in your prison of unhappiness.

I hope this book empowers you to go ahead and pursue your endeavours. If that is to become richer than Richard Branson, then so be it.

Let me show you what I know to be true: you can build a mountain of wealth and live a healthier lifestyle because you have what it takes and more.

I hope this book can be the starting point that helps you grow financially and become even more successful than ever before, so that you can pave the way for the next generations to come.

If you have picked up this book, you have decided that you do not want the fruit that has fallen from the tree (the easy choice). You want your own seeds to grow your own fruits for years to come, build value, and make an impact in your world.

One is hoping that the book enables you to redefine success for yourself and, as a result, gives you financial independence.

I don't say it lightly; if you want to grow and change your outcome in life and are wondering where to start, this book will give you the foundation you require to start building your wealth and make that change.

If you're trying to have a balanced life and stay true to your authentic self, whilst bringing up your children without feeling anxious, overburdened, or overwhelmed, then you're in the right place.

If you're feeling stuck living in the rat race and looking for a solid financial plan, this book could be your ticket to your freedom.

If you believe that your legacy is broken, this book will support you in overcoming and rebuilding the foundations, removing the curse that is holding you back.

Before I dive into the chapters, I want to give you my story and why I am so passionate about wealth building and a healthier lifestyle.

I am an empowerment coach. I empower ambitious single parents to help them fulfil their full potential.

But this wasn't always the case,

On one cold November day, I sat in the staff car park near the end of my lunch hour, shaking and crying uncontrollably because my body did not want to return to work.

A few weeks before that awful moment, my supervisor had called me into a small office with dimmed lights and chairs covered in blue cloth. The space was so tight; we just about managed to fit two chairs in there. We sat down face to face. His body leaned more towards the computer screen. I had to poke my head around to see the screen by twisting my chair to face the computer screen. At one point, I sat back, unbothered, about what he was looking at on the computer screen. He continued to tell me that his chart showed that I was not meeting the company's goals. To my surprise, I was never made aware of those particular goals. I was still in the learning stage, having just been with the team for less than a few months. He then asked me to sign a form without reading it. Me being me, I read the first line of the document and it said 'Performance Improvement Plan.' There was no representative from Human Resources present in the meeting, not even online.

I asked him why I was being put on a Performance Improvement Plan (PIP) and he replied that if I met the goals, then I would be removed from it immediately. I don't recall signing anything, but I was puzzled about the goals I had to meet.

You see, this was not the first time I had been put on a Performance Improvement Plan. This was the second time but at a different company. I recall the situation being so difficult that at one point, I saw myself diving into the nearby river. I am not a strong swimmer.

This situation was no different because my work environment changed. I went from the girl that was greeted every morning, to the one that everyone ignored or felt sorry for. Doing my work became increasingly difficult. I became nervous and shaky for no apparent reason. My smile was slowly fading, and my coping mechanism was to eat in expensive restaurants to escape my reality. Those who knew me well knew that I had a bubbly personality. My view of the world (including my workplace) was that everyone had a heart of gold. However, this view of people was again taken away from me.

I dreaded going to work and coming back to work after my lunch breaks. I was physically sick and just dragging my entire being into a space which made me feel unwanted.

One of my colleagues walked up to my car window on that cold November day. She asked me whether I was okay and I quickly said I was fine, but I was far from it. She was in the same team as me; I thought that telling her what I was going through would only feed her with information for her to gossip about amongst her friends. Paranoia became my best friend.

I was yet again a victim of bullying. Although my bosses and the company were different, I recognised the behaviour which made me feel like an outcast. You become familiar with this type of treatment when you have been bullied before.

I experienced this treatment at my last company. It was similar to when I had just arrived from Africa. In my primary school, my sisters and I were the minority. We were not only different in colour but also with our accents and expressions.

However, I knew how to stop bullying in primary school. I had to simply perform well in everything. From sports to music, being nice to everyone and following the rules. At work, the goalpost was different; my livelihood depended on it this time and to make matters worse, the goalpost was never defined clearly.

I was not told I was doing anything wrong during my time with this team or how I could improve in writing. I was not given any instructions on how to improve.

I was also never told how I would be supported to help me improve, how long the process would be, how and when it would be reviewed, and any possible outcomes. The meeting was with my supervisor, who was trying to hide the paperwork so that I could not read it.

I knew that being on a Performance Improvement Plan (PIP) meant I was closer to being fired again. The last time it happened, I had no idea what it was about, so I did everything I was told, although I felt anxious and uncomfortable.

This time it was different; I knew how this story could end for me. I was on edge, afraid and alone. I could not understand how the hell I could allow the same thing to happen to me again. In my mind, I was screaming: *"Why me, God? Again?!"*

I couldn't leave the company even when my mental health was affected. I had sleepless nights.

I knew the pain stemmed from the fact that I had no money to fall back on and no assets to create an income. My mind was too clouded to start looking for another job. Being an outcast took away my strength and positivity. I didn't even recognise myself in the mirror. Honestly, I am unsure how I managed to drive to and from work.

During this period, I was also a single mother and I had been granted special guardianship by court order for my niece, who was five years old. I was responsible for her welfare and emotional needs and I had to ensure that she had meaningful contact with her uncooperative parents.

I had to be strong and a positive role model for this little girl. Being on a Performance Improvement Plan (PIP) had me crumbling and questioning my purpose and existence. I often asked myself whether I was too nice or just plain stupid. I did not see my options, nor could I see my worth. I lost my happy smile.

The fear was real because I relied on that job for security and purpose. I had spent years in and out of welfare benefits and did not want to return there.

I have a 2:1 graded LLB (Hons) in Law degree and had the privilege of graduating from the best law school in London.

I had several interviews for many positions and employers said I was great in the interview but I either did not have enough experience or was overqualified. I did not want to become unemployed again. It was hard to secure a lucrative paying job. Whether in a recession or not, getting a job is difficult.

I finally found somewhere I felt comfortable. The salary was not great, but it was manageable. At work, I went from being praised for my amazing job (which encouraged me to support others, interpret policies and press the right buttons), to being told that those I supported were much more efficient and better at the job than I was.

The supervisor who always said 'good morning' to me no longer said it and my peers did not want to be seen talking to me out of fear that they would be next. They only approached me when the supervisor left the building.

I gathered my strength on one particular lunch break to join my colleagues in the staff canteen. Frankly, it was too cold to go outside and I did not have enough money to pay for a restaurant lunch.

Whilst eating my lunch, I overheard a co-worker from another team talking about how they were on a Performance Improvement Plan (PIP). They said they were going to the Union Representative to challenge it because it just didn't seem right.

I went to speak to the Union Representative just before my lunch hour had ended. My supervisor walked past whilst I was sitting and talking to them.

Fearfully, I ran to my desk, hoping he would not see me. He immediately came up to me and told me that I was no longer on a Performance Improvement Plan (PIP). This action confirmed to me that I had been bullied. The way he gave me the PIP was questionable even from the start, and the way it was removed was both unprofessional and did not adhere to the company's guidelines.

For instance, I was told in the meeting that I had to meet specific targets. That was the first time I heard that our team had those targets for those particular clientele groups. He did not state how I would be supported to meet those targets or how long the process would be. I was not given any review dates or a list of possible outcomes if I did not meet those targets.

I was not given the opportunity to have a representative with me. I now look back and see that this tactic was for me to leave the company. The tactics made me physically and mentally unstable. I did not go to the GP and dared not take any time off, and I felt that there was no one I could trust at my workplace. I couldn't leave because I thought my options were limited because of my past experiences looking for work.

Being told I was no longer on PIP, I realised I was financially unprepared. I had no savings for myself or for my daughter. I had allowed someone to have power over my livelihood. I also realised that success was not about having a great job or awards. It was about having freedom of choice, whether to stay, leave, or fight for that position. Without anything to fall back on, my options were limited this time around.

Therefore, I began my savings journey and as a result of this, I bought my first home. I managed to publish my father's books to fulfil his dream. On that journey, I discovered I could support others to achieve their full potential. I had known for years, but I could not put my finger on it until I analysed past and present events, as well as the awards and certifications I had. My transformation, changing future awards and my law background supported me and now, I have been transforming lives for over 15 years.

I never want anyone to feel the way that I felt, about their place of work. I don't want anyone to be financially unprepared. So, I devised the *Financial Empowerment Programme* to help those who want to fulfil their potential without worrying about where the resources will come from. It was about trusting that God will see you through as long as you put in the work.

The process will free you from societal slavery and make you a beacon of social hope for a beautiful life.

This is your guide to managing your finances and protecting your health physically, mentally, and spiritually, so that you can get on with the rest of your life.

The new era of technology is making it much easier for you to build wealth and improve your finances, allowing you to explore more options. More options also mean that you do not have to put up with working for people who make it the norm to bully others into meeting expectations that are sometimes unrealistic.

Your careers are not limited to the traditional 'Let me apply for a job and pray to get the job,' only to be ridiculed and threatened, instead of being treated as a human being.

Technology and the internet empower you and allow you to work with people worldwide.

Technology is allowing you to be able to create work. Due to technology and the internet, there is a global market so that you can produce and offer services to more people than ever before.

As money makers, you can become unstoppable; as a consumer, the world is your oyster.

Working mothers can now work from home. Remote working is not a new thing, but a thing that allows you to have more flexibility in life or the ability to work all around the world. It also helps you to get rid of old worries such as childcare costs or being late for a meeting when you can pop into a session on Zoom.

With the new advances, comes a new normal as you can quickly become a nomadic worker. People travel around the world and work using their laptops and Wi-Fi.

I knew a lady who had not worked for over five years, and she was so adamant that she could not work because of her depression and fear of working with others in a room. I later learned through my presentation that she was a queen at using technology and social media. She practically taught my class. She discovered her talent there and she could use it to earn extra cash.

As long as you have access to the internet and are open to learning new things to unleash the skills you have inside of you, then making money becomes easier and all you have to do now is learn how to manage it and make it work for you always.

I want to show you how your ideas can easily make you more prosperous. You never have to worry about competition from other businessmen and women. You too, can make money by being your unique self and sticking to the simple things in life.

Your vision should be a positive one. An example of a positive vision may lead you to solve your community's problems. To make that vision become a reality, you will have to take action by planning how to solve a particular problem. You then must create a system or a process by using your resources to make that vision a reality. Your source of income will come whilst you are serving the community. I hope you can use this book to guide you on how to produce and maintain the source of income you desire, so that it works for you and your legacy.

CHAPTER 1

Empower in Earning

" *If you think it, you can do it.*[3] "

How to make a million?
Firstly, you must know what a million looks like in numbers: £1,000,000.

Then, after knowing how much money you need in words and numbers, you have to divide it by how many people you need to serve to make a million.

This figure should give you an idea of the price tag that you need to price your goods and services to receive the one million for your hard work.

The more people you serve or, the higher the price tag, the more you can earn, it's that simple.

When you see footballers earning £100,000 in a week or a month, imagine how many people they are serving; how many people are buying the tickets to watch the match and how much they are being charged for each ticket. Yes,

---

3   Munroe, Dr. Myles (1991) *Understanding Your Potential: Discovering the Hidden You*, Destiny Image publishers Inc. Shippensburg, PA, p.102

it is one game, but that one game serves a packed venue. For instance, millions of people around the world watch Sky Television and pay extra to watch Match of the Day.

Let me give you another example:

If you sold a product/a programme/series or provided a service for £2,000 to 500 people, you would have accumulated a total of £1,000,000. This can be done in one day, several weeks, months or years. It depends on the price, what your offer is and the clientele you're serving.

To make a million pounds, you have to create a product or offer a service to people for a fee. The product and price tag can change, depending on you. The clients are only concerned about the results they can get and the transformation you will make in their lives.

The key to successfully making that million over and over again is to provide excellent services and products to your customers. You must also ask for the price that your product and services are worth so that your customers can keep pouring into you regularly. If they know that you are a great servant and provide more than just that one-off service, that will speak volumes.

An example I am going to give you is from my Coach Patrice Washington. She charges a fee for her course of about $3,000 and serves thousands of women offering the best value for money. As a result, it is guaranteed you will come back and continue pouring into her because she pours into your cup and leaves you wanting more.

By the time you finish her course, you will have transformed both mentally and financially. When I completed the *Command the Stage Programme* and delivered my presentation, I was surprised by the amount of people that were interested in my services. They were also not afraid to find the money to learn.

The example above is not the only way to make a million, but it's a good example that you can try. The illustration is there to help you to start thinking of creative ways to increase your income.

Have finer things in life

Perhaps you want to have the latest iPhone when it has just been released. You may wish to travel around the world or start your own business. Being financially empowered is the ability to be able to pay for your wants and needs without over-stretching yourself.

So, why have you not started to earn that million and beyond yet (assuming that you are earning less than a million)?

In my honest opinion, it's because you have never been taught how to. If you don't know, you just don't know, and if you are not inquisitive enough, then you will never know.

We are not exposed to the reality of how finances really work in the real world. Financial literacy is not taught at school because teachers have been trained to teach only curriculum subjects. It is not even included in Personal Social Health Education (PSHE) lessons. How do you explain to a child that even if you earn £100,000 per month, you may still be poor if you overspend?

Schools use basic examples which make no difference to a person's livelihood. For instance, they would teach you maths and use an example of three apples times two apples equal six apples. They do not explore bigger and more advantageous examples, such as three houses times two equals six houses, which you could rent out to increase your income streams. If you rent out six houses for £1000 per month, you would have £6,000 per month before tax.

If you think in apples, all you are going to do is buy apples, but if you think in houses, you are more likely to want to buy houses in the future. At this level of thinking, you are already shifting that child's mindset.

Whilst teachers can't teach our children everything, they can try to connect the dots between what would be profitable for the community and what is unprofitable.

Some of us are not taught financial literacy at home either for various reasons, and the most common one is the fact that parents are often too busy earning money and do not have time to talk it.

My parents worked endless days and nights doing all sorts of manual jobs to pay the bills and feed us. They never had that much time with us during the day because they were too tired. My parents never had the time to sit down and read bedtime stories to us, and they never checked our homework. It was literally left to us as children to do the homework and get ourselves to school on time.

Learning how to deal with finances is directly connected to how our parents or caregivers dealt with money in front of us. I believe we are a product of our environment, especially at a young age. This also includes what we watched on TV and what the media portrayed at the time.

If the media reported on prosperity, you would behave differently from someone who has grown up with a press that focused on financial depression and austerity measures.

I would like you to think back to when you were a child. You may need to close your eyes and think back to the first time you heard about money.

- Did you hear people telling you that they did not have enough money?
- Did you get whatever you wished for?
- Were there any fights about money or bills?
- Who paid for your clothes?
- Did you wear the latest fashion trends in school, and who bought those outfits?
- Do you remember the first time you held cash in your hands?

Think back to what was said about money, how it was handled, and how it made you feel.

- Were you happy, or did it make you feel sad?
- Did you get a job when you were young and what was your reason for getting that job?
- Do you remember any conversation about money?
- Do you still hold the same beliefs today?

Write down your answers to those questions. Then go back to the answers you have given. Can you spot a pattern? If you cannot spot a pattern, then it might help if you do the exercise with a trusted friend. Let them analyse your responses. Can they see a pattern with how you deal with your finances now and how that pattern is connected to your past?

After doing this exercise, you should see that your habits and thoughts with money are generational and stem from your past experiences as a child.

Your job now is to decide whether that habit or behaviour is supporting your purpose or hindering your prosperity. And if it's not helping you to fulfil your life's purpose then the next step to take is to try and create new positive habits that will help you prosper to replace the old unwanted habits or thoughts about money that are hindering your growth.

Before you start taking those positive steps, you first must forgive yourself and anyone who gave you the wrong advice and any negative views you encountered as a child.

1. It was not their fault because this was all they knew.
2. It was never your fault either because you were too young to understand and seek the truth.
3. Forgive the past because forgiveness will set you free and leave room for positive growth.

The majority of us end up seeking to work a 9-5 to pay the bills and nothing beyond that because that is all we know. By the time we realise that we want more in life than just paying the bills, we are too scared to take risks and step into the unknown.

Especially if you have experienced being unemployed and struggled to get your current job in the first place.

Because we are too frightened to lose what we have, we end up limiting ourselves in doing what is familiar and we end up living a life that admires those who have managed to achieve beyond what we can imagine.

We start calling them the lucky ones but guess what? You too might become the lucky one if you apply the principles in this book, to your life.

As an outsider, I assumed that the education system is governed by what is on offer and prepares youngsters to serve the needs of its environment. For example, I went to a sixth form college with my daughter. I felt that there was a lot of indirect pushing that the administrators did to gear young adults toward studying social care, especially if you did not get the grades to do what you liked.

I assumed that this was purely based on the economic needs of the community not on what the child wants to do. At the time of writing this book, there was a huge drive to have more carers in the local community and you saw buses advertising for adult social carers, stating '...needs you.' These adverts were a direct response to an increasing elderly population who need support in the communities. There is absolutely nothing wrong with that, however, we have to also accept that not everyone can do this type of work - you need a heart and mind that is naturally gifted to care for people.

We are not all equipped in the same way. Forcing someone to do something they are not equipped for can cause more harm than good. There is nothing wrong in doing work for the time being in order to get the job you really want, but to do work that you have very little drive for is damaging to the soul, and you will probably be less productive in the role which could damage your self-esteem.

You are far less likely to be encouraged to create work and become a leader, unless you came from an elite group, have connections, or are privileged from birth. The honest truth of the matter is that if you come from a working-class background and happened not to achieve the grades, you are left with whatever government-funded courses are on offer at the colleges who deliver the governments' agenda.

If you look at the individuals who went to schools such as Eton, the children in those schools are economically connected in private and public sectors. This is not to say that they have financial literacy skills, but this is to acknowledge the fact that even if they failed, are out of luck with money, and did not make the grades, they would have a friendly connection who would offer them work and be willing to train them to do the job. Having connections can pave many ways for you.

When I worked for a commercial bank, I recall asking a few of my white colleagues how they secured their positions. Most of them admitted that a friend of a friend assisted, whilst my black colleagues on the flip side asked me how I got my job.

The amount of time, energy, pressure, education, and money you may spend in asking employers for work, plus the amount of rejection you might experience, could easily equal that same amount of energy, time, and capital you use to start your own business. If one is not hiring you, I always say why not hire yourself? Keep your options open with the goal to earn more than you did yesterday.

The power of earning is within you. However, you may be surrounding yourself with lies and half-told truths and have naturally become stuck, depressed, and angry, if not anxious and worried. I honestly believe that prejudicial behaviour, jealousy, and envy, stem from a lack of knowledge. That lack of knowledge impacts on your ability to work out how to increase your earnings, save money and live your best life.

When we get it wrong

Why education is key to knowledge but not necessarily the key to wealth creation.

Basic education is absolutely crucial, and it should be a must for everyone. In the UK, basic education is free to all, although not everyone takes advantage of its value due to their life circumstances. It is valuable and a key to a great start in life.

However, the missing ingredient is the ability for basic education to be taught in a way that mirrors real life experiences that your children will encounter as they get older. For example, the fact that learning numbers is required to be able to count your money to pay the bills, or to purchase that car your parent is driving to get you to school.

We get basic education and that is what it is, basic. Little effort is made to connect the learning with the realities of the learners. One reason is that there is not enough time in the classes and perhaps lack of suitable resources. Students are left to connect the dots which is not always easy because the connection is not prominent, or we remain fixated in the present and have little time to plan for the future.

> 66 *Keep your options open with the goal to earn more than you did yesterday.*

Have you ever had a child saying: *"Why do I have to learn maths?"* or *"why do I have to read every day?"* This is an opportunity to explain and connect the lessons learnt to reality so that the child can be encouraged to develop their skills.

For example, during a trip to Uganda, I had the opportunity to have a chat with my 15-year-old niece and she told me that she did not like physics and that she struggled with it. She did not see the point of learning about the properties.

I admitted to her that I for one, never understood the subject until I got older. I wish that I was told, in order to create my hair products, I have to understand the physical elements in the hair product, and in order to create the best cream for my skin I needed to know the properties that make up the cream.

Failing to make the deeper connection leaves us with gaps in our knowledge and understanding on how things work. For example, the biggest gaps in our learning are:

1. Financial literacy
2. How to communicate with customers and serve them well
3. The economy and how it affects the home and the wider environment

So, when situations such as the increase in gas prices, petrol and inflation occurs, people are not so surprised and are able to adapt and adjust according to their environment. We all have the potential to earn a lot more money; technology and its advances has made this even more possible. You have to take advantage of it - the quicker you learn, the faster you can make a lot of money and continue to live in your given purpose.

The traditional route of going to school and getting a great job that pays well is fantastic when you are highly paid and are able to meet the cost of living. On the face of it, you would seem successful in other people's eyes. However, one of the things, that I wish I knew when job hunting is that I had several options:

- To start a business serving people
- To create useful products and sell them to other people (this should be widely encouraged)
- To become an apprentice
- To apply for internships
- To apply for traineeships
- To volunteer in an area that interests you
- To apply to college or university

Education

Education is the key to knowledge - that is a fact. The lie you have been taught is that the more you learn, the more you earn. We have been feeding ourselves a lie and it has led some of us to become stuck in the learning process. Some of us do not know how to convert that learning into productivity to generate the kind of income we want. We are not even guaranteed a high paying job. It's clearly a lie but we continue to believe in it, so much so that most of us are willing to get into a lot of debt consuming education.

This is the reason why I spent years studying law and accumulating student loan debt and then paying on top, for law school. I passed, but there are many individuals that I know that failed miserably and many of them were from ethnic minority groups. I honestly remember a lot of my black peers arguing about their results. I recall one of the tutors stating, *"The system was not designed for ethnic minorities because everyone has different learning styles."* The truth of the matter is that we all have different learning styles as individuals and it is not based on whether we come from a particular ethnic background.

She actually gave pupils a separate class to support those students and used diagrams and colours. This was very kind of her, but nobody could hide the fact that those students who were in her extra classes she gave for free, kept on getting bad results and were predominantly Asian and Black students.

We also have to consider the fact that even before we had completed our exams, a lot of my white peers in my class had secured training contracts and they all passed the exams first time round. It looked like the chances of an ethnic minority student passing the exams seemed very slim and even slimmer in securing a training contract.

In one of my exams, I was sure that I had answered all the questions on the exam paper with confidence and expected to score a high mark of at least 80%. However, I was awarded 50% as the pass mark and although I was happy to have passed the exam, I felt disappointed with the marks I received.

There are plenty of law students who make it in this field and plenty of others that don't. From my experience, I found that the key to educational success or even to get further than merely just obtaining a degree especially for ethnic minorities is to:

1. Have a clear understanding of how the education system works and what is expected of you on that course and in the work environment before embarking on it.
2. Get networking with those that are working in the area that you wish to specialise in.
3. Be prepared to develop your qualifications, for example obtaining a Master's or a Doctorate degree. This will give you a head start, and you will not be easily overlooked as you will most likely be overqualified for plenty of positions.

Will you become a millionaire or a billionaire taking the educational route?

No, I don't really know anyone who became a billionaire by getting a Master's degree.

However, a pattern that I have noticed through my years of observation is that education is not a guarantee for success, but good for knowledge that you can use to support yourself and your communities. What good is knowledge if you cannot use it to enrich yourself as well as others?

Imagine this, you go to school, pass your GCSEs and A-levels, and then you apply to go to university where you are required to pay university fees which go up every year.

If you want to study medicine or law, you will also have to pay a professional studies fee which you don't have. You decide to do it anyway, in hopes that you will get a high-paying job once it is completed.

Only to get out and struggle to get a job, not only to pay for your living expenses but to pay off the loans and overdrafts and credit cards which you took out to pay for the courses and living expenses.

For many of us who took that route, starting off with no money in our accounts meant that we got into deficits even before we got our first jobs. We were already in debt even before we even started earning.

When you start off life in debt, it puts you in a vulnerable position and you can easily be exploited. One could say that you are living just below the poverty line. You become a slave to your masters, the companies, corporations, and organisations, and you often accept a job you probably do not want because you need to pay off the loans.

Information on government student loans or professional studies loans and how much to pay back, and when it can be written off (for UK Citizens) is on www.gov.uk. The amount paid back depends on your income.

Student bank loans are offered to students by banks in the form of student credit cards, overdrafts and student bank accounts to help with living expenses; student loans from the government department may be paid into your chosen student bank account that has perks like student discounts and overdraft etc. to entice you to open an account with them.

If you want to become financially independent and have more options in life, you would have to earn way above the threshold set out by the government to start paying back the loans.

Earning more will allow you to repay the loans accumulated while studying.

Earning above any threshold will remove the earning scale someone else has set out for you.

Earning above the threshold would remove any scarcity mindset (that tells you, that you can't make any more than that) you may have unintentionally created in your mind.

Earning more than the threshold would increase your options and have you living a life of abundance, not just below the poverty line.

Earning more will empower you to acknowledge that there are no limits on how much you can achieve in life.

Why work towards someone's standards of wealth for you when you can be more than what you are right now? ⁇

After getting the qualifications, your intention is to apply for a job in the field that you have studied in. Competition in most work fields is fierce so to get a job becomes almost a miracle in itself. A few make it through, but others will start getting rejection letters one after the other and each one is bound to knock your confidence, little by little.

It's almost as if the system is built to suppress us into becoming like slaves on earth. We end up being at the mercy of companies and employers and industries because we are now in need of money to feed ourselves and our children, and at the same time we are under pressure from society to meet all these milestones such as getting married, have children, buying a house and cars.

You then start working in fields you've never studied, chasing wealth and leaving your natural talents and purpose behind. The only thing you have to show, is a certificate saying how well you have managed and completed your tasks.

There is nothing wrong with getting certificates because it shows that you able to complete tasks - this is perceived as a great skill to have, and it shows that one has resilience and can get to an end goal. However, it's even better when you can be rewarded adequately for your talent because after all, money buys bread.

I am not sure if you have ever applied for a job, but it's like marketing yourself with your skills and qualities you have to offer the organisation or company. In my experience, there is no adequate preparation for this at school or in adult education colleges and universities.

Career services offer written scripts in the career you said you would like to get into, and they leave it up to you to go and act.

Before getting paid work, you will need to create a curriculum vitae (CV), make an application, go for interviews and then be on probation for three to six months. This is a marketing skill that you must learn, to be able to stand out and beat the competition.

I clearly lacked the marketing skill for the fact that I was in and out of the job centre for years before I landed a permanent role. The bank chased me for money whilst I chased jobs. It was easier for me to get a retail post than in office or law films. I even tried volunteering at the Citizen Advice Bureau which taught me a great deal about dealing with debt and community problems, but I was never good enough for employers or to be hired within the bureau itself. This of course always came down to funding issues... the struggle was real.

The Evening Standard stated that in 2018-2019, 56% of U.K. domiciled graduates were in full time employment. I am sure there are other factors to take into consideration but for the amount of fees one pays to get qualified, we should expect that 75% of those who graduate should be in full time employment, not including those who went to travel after graduating.

When I was applying to law firms, I received a call from a friend who had gone to law school with me. She told me that she had made over 100 applications for a training contract and had only received one offer for an interview. My soul sunk and I wondered what hope I had.

Due to lack of knowledge about what I was able to do with my skills and massive self-doubt, that dreaded imposter syndrome kept telling me I was not good enough. I drifted ashore for a long time. I hope that you can avoid this experience and the pitfalls that I went through, so that you can make money much faster than I did, without losing yourself and your purpose.

We are at times bombarded with images that are fake. These images can be a catalyst to your vision, for a better life or a better place. If you don't have the faith and belief that you too can have those nice things, by working on your purpose, then you are more likely to struggle with getting paid your worth. An empty faith leads to an empty palm.

I recall my time at law school in which I joined a Black law society. I attended one of their functions. This is where I first saw my friend Cornelius, a pretty young black woman who gave an amazing presentation. She was stunning and spoke eloquently.

I really thought that she would bag herself a training contract only to learn years later that she felt used for show and that no one offered her any training contracts, or even a paralegal position. She was actually still hunting whilst working night shifts as a care worker.

Her image being on stage made me feel like I could also do this but that's what it was, an image. Her reality was different from the image she portrayed on stage. Many of us are given these images to make us believe that we too can make it. So, we try, only to find out it was all a facade. One thing I know is that all is not hopeless, when you operate in your purpose.

Sometimes, it's also about who you know.

On one occasion, one of my white friends said in conversation that she also found it hard to get work. She said that she only managed to secure her first job because her mother knew someone who worked for a solicitor's firm who had agreed to take her on.

Whilst working at a corporate bank. I met a young white guy, who was around 20 years old, and I asked him how he got into working for the bank. He replied that he got a call from his friend's uncle about a position that was available. The rest was history - his starting salary was £50,000.

What sometimes makes it more difficult to be hired are the so-called human biases in the people that are hiring, who invalidate your credibility. Your qualifications then become invalid because one cannot compete when there are biases against your ethnicity, gender, sexual orientation, disability, or social background. It is therefore wise to learn how to navigate the unfair system, so that you may prosper and live a happier life.

The economic market can also be the reason as to why some people make more money whilst others struggle to see the opportunities. Understanding what the market trends are in any particular season for your industry is crucial to be able to earn more, and do more, even in bad times.

Never stop learning. Knowledge is power and it is necessary, although it is not the only key to financial freedom.

Whenever you receive a rejection letter from companies and other organisations remember that a NO means 'new opportunities' (something I learnt from Patrice Washington).

The truth is that even when you have no formal education, you can multiply your income. Success is available for most people, if you learn how to tap into your zone of genius, like this young lady did, Victoria Molyneux. Victoria has created a mega business online called *Want That Trend*. She never obtained any GCSEs and she stated that her teachers thought that she would never amount to anything.

Whilst on maternity leave from her telesales job, Victoria, started to research the power of social media and how to use it, before starting her company. She started off small and now is an award-winning businesswoman worth over a million. Her success started off as a vision, before taking action to make it her reality. She has paved the way for many people who do not have an education and have been told that they will never amount to anything.

What are your ideas? Do not sit on your vision, go out and serve! If she can do it, so can you.

Another illustration of a person who was at his lowest point in his life, with just an idea and a mindset shift: Richard LeMieux. He is living proof that shows that even when you are at your lowest point in life, you can still turn your knowledge and the little you have into wealth. Richard lost his home and family and as a result, he ended up on the streets homeless. Whilst he was homeless, he wrote a book *Breakfast with Sally* which made him an author as well as a public speaker on the subject of homelessness.

I believe that no matter what circumstance or situation you are facing at present, you too have the potential to earn extra money. Don't let fear or doubt stop you from becoming who you ought to be, and in many respects, this also includes those in third world countries such as Uganda. The potential is within you and it may take hitting rock bottom to ignite the ability inside of you.

On my trip to Uganda in 2018, one thing I realised is that there were a lot of street vendors ranging from young children, adults and those who were disabled selling various products from food to watches. Not everyone can be an entrepreneur (some may say), but when push comes to shove, we can all sell something to survive.

You may not even need a business, sales or marketing degree. When times are hard, people become enterprising to survive. The entrepreneur within wakes up. Why wait to be desperate or to be pushed on the edge to find ways to earn?

Most of us, have the ability to create our own work. Do we all want to be entrepreneurs? Perhaps not, not all of us want to work for ourselves and that is okay too, as long as you're happy and feel content within yourself.

How do we know that we have the ability to create our own work? For some people it may take working for other people and in time seeing that there are problems in this world that could easily be solved. You start to feel as though you are just not a great fit for that company you're working for, or that something is missing.

It may be that you have tried to open up your own business and failed numerous times due to mismanagement of your finances, but the entrepreneur spirit is still burning inside of you.

A friend of mine told me how he started his security company. He said that it was the amount of disrespect and bureaucracy that he faced working for an employer, that pushed him to start his own company. He has never regretted becoming his own boss.

I would say that being an entrepreneur is not an easy route. Therefore, ask questions, learn from those who have failed and those who have survived. Take note of your own failures as well as those things that you have done well. Most of all, have patience and determination and be clear on what the customer needs and wants. Always also be ready to serve.

The most important thing which can help you on your journey to entrepreneurship or when you're chasing purpose is to have money saved up. This might mean working for other people until you have enough resources to support your business.

The power of social media as a tool to generate incredible wealth

Social media is a powerful tool that can be used to generate incredible wealth because it allows you to reach out virtually to a global community. This is where you might be able to get the 500 customers to buy your product for £2,000 to make you a millionaire.

The plus side is that social media does not discriminate, and everyone has their own audience. You may get a set of people that may not like you, but another set might love you and want more from you. You have to remember that to be empowered to earn more, you have to serve many people. Just like some footballers do when they play in stadiums full of thousands of people.

A business online costs less than most offline businesses because the overheads are small. It might just take you, your vision, your gift, and your passion for you to start that business.

YouTube is an incredible platform that you can use to market yourself and once you get over a particular number of viewers watching your videos, you are actually paid to continue using the platform.

According to *influencermarketinghub.com/youtube-views-to-make-money*:

> "*YouTube can be a very lucrative way to earn money, but you'll first need to have at least 1,000 subscribers and 4,000 watched hours over the last 12 months before you can start thinking about monetizing your videos. Once you have reached this milestone, you can apply for the YouTube Partner Program and receive ads on your videos. According to Digiday, YouTube*

creators with more than 100,000 subscribers can earn about $2,000 per video."[4]

Platforms like Tik Tok, Instagram, Pinterest, Facebook, Twitter and Snapchat can also be used to gain potential clients and can also be monetised.

Using these tools are a great way to grow your earnings and have fun at the same time. It is essential to learn how to use the platforms in a way that is comfortable for you and grow your audience organically.

A single mum of two told me that she was finding it difficult to find work as well as look after her children. I recommended that she should look into creating her own business online, that would allow her flexibility and maybe even cut out the childcare cost and travel. I directed her to the *Want That Trend* website as an example. This was an eye opener for her because she spent hours on these platforms to reach out to family and friends. Now, she knew that she was able to use social media to potentially generate wealth and still be able to look after her family.

I genuinely believe that technology is the definite game changer. It has produced a new era, making the impossible even more possible, making it possible for most people to reach new heights in the realm of success in their area of interest and purpose not just in any field.

---

4   Influence marketing Hub, (2022) "How Many YouTube Views Do You Really Need to Make Money". [online] Available at: *influencermarketinghub.com/ youtube-views-to-make-money* [Accessed 20 November 2022].

Literally no one is left behind. If you are disabled or have other circumstances that you feel are hindering you, just simply telling your story about your situation in words, pictures or videos can open new avenues for you and make you more money than ever before.

The social media community love people who are genuinely themselves and the power of being able to tell your story on how you have survived a situation is wonderful. You can help others do the same and you might even save someone's life just by telling your story.

During my time as a personal adviser for over 13 years and with my experience being in and out of the job market, the one thing I always say to anyone seeking work is:

"If no one is hiring you, don't worry because you can always hire yourself," and social media allows us to do just that.

Welcome to the rat race

I worked for a public sector company and one day we were in a meeting when the head of that company asked us how we felt about our working conditions. He seemed happy and eager to get honest feedback, so a few confident people expressed their discontentment on how things were done and how it actually made them feel. His response was: *"If you do not like the job then leave."* Then he said that, he would leave if he was not happy. I looked at him with disbelief and all the senior staff echoed the same sentiments. I was disappointed in their behaviour. I can see now that this was done intentionally to drive people out of the company. The aim was to make people leave the company so that they don't have to offer them full severance package.

The truth is, most people would probably leave if they were unhappy in their positions. If they were aware of the options available to them and were financially prepared. But some people are caught up in the rat race, living paycheque to paycheque. This is when you're earning just enough to pay the bills and to take care of your children (if you have any).

Patrice Washington said it best in her programme *Platform to Purpose* that I joined in 2021. She found that many people are so grateful to have a job in the first place and may have prayed for that job, that they put up with unfair behaviour to keep the job. I would add that so many people have mismanaged their finances that they feel there is no other option but to stay in a job that pays their bills.

Working in an unhappy workplace can result in developing mental health issues, depression, anxiety, a sense of failure and a gradual loss of life purpose.

This was me at one point. I had been so grateful for this job because it provided security, that I held on to it and put up with abuse time and time again. It was not only destroying my soul but also eating away at my confidence little by little, turning me into a bitter and ungrateful person.

I know people who even contemplated suicide because they could see no way out of the rat race. Are you one of them? If so, I want you to know that life is not always black and white - you are here on Earth for a purpose, and it is not to be abused. God has a plan for you, you just have to trust in Him whilst seeking support.

We have a plan

If you do not like your job then prepare to escape. Do everything with the intention that if you're fired or are politely asked to leave, you are prepared for the exit and can survive at least three to six months without any income coming in. Create an emergency fund account and label it 'new opportunities' and start growing it. This will be covered in Chapter Four in more detail.

What you do not want to do is stick around long enough to be abused mentally and tortured indirectly because that could leave you traumatised for life, unable to operate in your greatness and damage your well-being.

The problem with being at the mercy of someone else is that they can feed you anything and you will take it and one of them is to make you believe that you're not enough.

According to David Bach, in his book *Smart Women Finish Rich*, he stated that if you find yourself underpaid, underappreciated, or underdeveloped in your career or business, you should find somewhere else to go.[5]

My father Ham Kaima also stated in his book *My Arrogant friends – The rise and Fall and Fall of Uganda* that "*Getting a job is everybody's success, doing it well*

---

5   Bach, D., (2018) *Smart Women Finish Rich- 8 Steps to achieving Financial Security and Funding Your Dreams*. 2nd Edition. United States: Currency (CurrencyBooks.com) p.337

is an achievement and being loved by your boss is an additional joy. Similarly, working under pressure and hatred is tantamount to a voluntary entry into hell".[6]

That employer might tell you lies that you are not good enough because you happen not to meet their benchmark but that is simply not true, because you are more than enough for God or else you would have never been born in the first place.

The quicker you acknowledge that you were put on the Earth for a reason and not just to please your boss, the better. You need to stop being afraid of failing and embrace rejection. Being rejected is a clear sign that you need to evaluate your situation and tap into your gifts and your zone of genius.

A positive idea that massively serves individuals will always get God's blessings accordingly. Let me tell you once again, you're more than enough because you have untouched resources at your disposal.

You are more than enough

Before you dive into the plan, I would like you to acknowledge this fact that you have the resources to fulfil your full potential in life and that you are more than enough.

You are more than enough, to turn yourself into an incredible money-making machine. Only if you dare to open your eyes and see the many resources God has provided for

---

6   Kaima, H., (2022) *My Arrogant Friends- The Rise and Fall and Fall of Uganda.* JoeNeDoe Company U.K: p16

you. Whether you consider yourself poor or rich, everything you need to start walking into your purpose is within your reach.

In his book *Releasing your Potential- Exposing the Hidden You*, Dr Myles Munroe stated: *"The wealth of your resources is limitless if you will allow God to open your eyes to their possibilities... Change your thinking to 'I need more mentality' and use what you already have."*[7]

He outlines six principles in his book:

1. God makes and provides for all people. Some become rich and some become poor.
2. Wealth and poverty are primarily based on what you do with what you have.
3. God gives you resources to live on, not for.
4. The proper use of resources releases potential.
5. The improper use (abuse) of resources kills potential.
6. You have many resources that you aren't presently using.

One of the resources we have are our mouths.

In Rabia Lapin's book, *Business Secrets from the Bible*: he shares: *"All business professionals, good communication skills are what make the difference between earning a lot*

---

7 Munroe, Dr Myles, (2002) *Releasing your Potential- Exposing the Hidden You*, Published in Partnership - Destiny Image and The Diplomat Press, Nassau, Bahamas, p. 136

of money and little money. Speech is God's great gift to us. It's a unique gift that God gave to humans."[8]

"Whether you're a waiter, plumber, bookkeeper, veterinarian, or landscaper, whatever you do for a living, you will perform better and make more money if you learn to use your mouth more effectively than you do now."[9]

He then goes on to say that: *"The mouth is a vital tool that takes us from slavery to freedom. It is a vital tool to move from darkness into light."*[10]

A classic example of a person who used his mouth to make a living is Les Brown, one of the world's best motivation speakers. He was called 'mentally retarded' at a very young age, but later on in life, he found the power of communication by using his mouth. He earns more than $25,000 per hour for public speaking. If he can do it, then so can you.

I also use my mouth to tell my story of how I discovered the six principles. I use my mouth to conduct group sessions to help other people discover their full potential in life and to also conduct presentations.

I am also booked to give talks on personal finance and wellbeing. Through practice and attending courses such as *Command the Stage,* and *Toastmasters,* I have been able to

8   Lapin, Rabbi D. (2014) *Business Secrets from the Bible: Spiritual Success Strategies for Financial Abundance,* New Jersey/Canada: Wiley, p. 147

9   ibid.

10 Lapin, Rabbi D. (2014) *Business Secrets from the Bible: Spiritual Success Strategies for Financial Abundance,* New Jersey/Canada: Wiley, p.199

improve on my skills. If you feel as though you too can do this, then I will urge you to start with reading out loud to yourself at home for over 20 minutes per day and joining courses.

66 *Whether you consider yourself poor or rich, everything you need to start walking into your purpose is within your reach.*

You can either misuse the gift that God gave you by just talking for the sake of it or learn to use it properly to engage with other people and help your community by speaking positive words. Eventually, people will ask you to come and speak on stages for a nice fee.

Look at the palm of your hands. What are you holding in your hands? Could it be a mobile phone with internet? That phone could be that one resource you need to create another source of income. If you use your resources the way the resources were intended to be used, you could potentially earn more than you do right now.

Another example of resources being used for its purpose, is the time when my father was put on palliative care. He was given four weeks to live, but he told me he had three months. I worked intensively for four weeks to help him accomplish his dream of publishing his last book and fulfil his purpose by helping him type it - *The Talking Snake*. We used the same laptop and when I finished typing it, he then checked for any mistakes.

All of a sudden, my laptop screen stopped working whilst we were in the middle of doing the work. It took a month to get the screen fixed.

I had to think first. I then decided to use the resource I had, which was an old Mac that had not been used for a while. I then asked him to continue his work on that computer. He was reluctant because it meant that he had to learn to use a new keyboard and he knew that time was not on his side.

Myself and my daughter Robyn, took the time to show him the keys and he learnt them and continued to type. He eventually completed his book on that Mac before he sadly passed away on 11ᵗʰ August 2022.

I managed to help my father fulfil his full potential by ensuring that his book was completed using the resources that were available at the time. His ideas were typed on paper for the world to read before he passed away.

I understand that at times you may not be able to see the resources that you have or the potential you have inside of you. Therefore, you may need to hire a coach to help you with this, perhaps an empowerment coach. I help people like yourself reach their full potential in life and become a high performer.

Now that you have established that you are more than enough and have more than enough resources to tap into to earn more money, let's dive into our purpose. Trust me; this will help you with your earning power.

Patrice Washington states as one of her mantras that we should chase purpose and not money in her redefining wealth community. This is my coach from the *Purpose to Platform* and *Command the Stage* programmes and I am so proud to be part of this purpose-chasing community.

I genuinely believe in this mantra: 'chase purpose and not money' because purpose-chasing is much more fulfilling in life whether you are making millions or just striving to fulfil your full potential.

During the 2008 recession, I was one of the many people to have left the bank I was working at. I wanted to look for work that paid me the same salary or above. Until I got a phone call from one of the Vice Presidents at that bank, encouraging me to get any job. I listened, and I then started to hand out my CV around Oxford Street. Weeks later, I ended up working for Karen Millen, a retail shop.

On my first day of work, on that particular morning, I got out of bed, had a bath, put on my makeup and looked into the mirror. I felt content and this was a moment of joy for me. I began to feel more confident. I didn't care about how much I was getting paid anymore.

The idea of being able to get up and serve others gave me purpose. The feeling I felt inside is what drove me to go and work in a place that was too far from my home and paid me just above the minimum wage. My heart was open to new opportunities and new ideas. Just having that hope helped my well-being.

Right there and then, I understood what chasing purpose meant; when you pursue purpose, you are moving towards your destiny and what you are called to do in life. You will know it is your purpose because you will be fulfilled even when you don't have a lot of money. The driving force is not money, it's your wellbeing.

In the book *Rich Dad Poor Dad*, Robert Kiyosaki, taught us to use jobs as learning tools, not a place for life. He stated: *"I recommend to young people to seek work for what they will learn, more than what they will earn."*[11]

He worked in many positions such as in sales and marketing, which taught him a great deal so when it came to selling his book, he knew how to market himself. He did not have to be the best writer in the world.

There are several jobs that Robert recommended that we should all try, which will help us in our businesses or the near future such as: sales; marketing; accounting and communication. He also advised that we should learn more than one language, if possible. Never be afraid to venture out and move from one area of work to another to learn.

If you do not know what your purpose, gift or passion is in life, getting any work might help you find it, because you are then exposed to all kinds of situations that will prepare you, or give you ideas as to what you can do, or what you definitely do not want to do.

Here is the plan which could start you off on the road to earning:

Plan A - If you have no cash, then get any work. Please do not get caught up in the process and rejection. Just do it - this is called 'in the meantime stage.'

---

11 Kiyosaki, R T. (2017) Rich *Dad Poor Dad*, 3rd Edition – 20th Anniversary edition, United States of America: Plata Publisher. LLC p. 201

Plan B - Whilst in plan A - start looking for the work you wish to do, or you would like to do. That work may even be in the job you are in. When ideas come into your head about how to solve a problem, or an issue write them down. Write down the problems you see at work and how you can best solve them. It doesn't matter if people will not listen to you - formulate the plan and learn how to execute it with or without your company.

Plan C - Whilst doing plan A and B, use some of the money you're earning to save. The more you save, the better. This is for you to prepare for your dream and purpose - the money is for new opportunities because once you find out what you are destined to do, you may need the resource to start the company. You will need capital to fund that big dream. You do not want to have to beg anyone to fund your dreams. Save for new opportunities because they will come up.

If you are in a crisis, a recession or pandemic, you can still find new opportunities, and as Dr Myles Munroe stated: *"In the Chinese language there is no word for crisis; it's called opportunity – you say you have a crisis, they say you have an opportunity..."*[12]

---

12 EG Siyaga, (2021) Dr Myles Munroe On Chinese Secret For Dominion *youtube.com/watch?v=inx-QBPjTpQ* (*Uniform Resource Locator*) *[20/11/2022]*.

I came across an interview that Oprah Winfrey did with Robert Kiyosaki titled *How to become Rich!!!*[13] She had interviewed one of the guys who had taken Robert's advice and put it into practice. He stated that he used his job to save up some money and start his home-based business which cost him less than $300 to create. He then used that money from his job to buy real estate and within a year, his income had risen from $48,000 a year to $100,000.

How to strengthen your earning power

The way to strengthen your earning power is to have passive multiple streams of income.

Passive income is income that you earn, that does not require you to be there physically, leaving you to get on with your life or work another job.

It gives you options and having that freedom increases your confidence and self-esteem. It's the automatic power in the earning strategy that we should try to adhere to.

For three reasons:

1. You will have a system that generates money over and over again without you being present.
2. You can increase your income bracket by increasing your prices to how much money you want to make according to the season and what's possible.

---

13 *Amanda Smith*, (2014). Oprah interviewing: Robert Kiyosaki: [YouTube], Available at: *facebook.com/watch/?v=345673923348135* (Accessed 10.01.2023)

3. It gives you freedom of choice and your time and space back, which you can use to enjoy life and give back to the less fortunate.

If you want to fulfil your full potential in life today, then go to *sandrakaima.com*

and sign up to the mailing list. You can get free resources that will help you on your journey to fulfilling your full potential.

66 *The way to strengthen your earning power is to have passive multiple streams of income.*

CHAPTER 2

Empower in Spending

> ❝ *Even the rich have limits.*[14] ❞

This quote had me thinking of the many things I want and need. If I vigorously pursued them all, I would have no savings for the things that are important to me, which are the things that make me happy and keep me whole and balanced.

In fact, I realised unending spending leads to a life of endless misery. How you spend your money reflects who you will become.

In order to live your purpose, you have to become empowered in how you spend money.

You need to limit your spending to only those things that serve you well. Save the rest for the many opportunities you cannot foresee in your current circumstances but will soon be your present.

---

14 Clason S. George. (2015) *The Richest Man In Babylon*. Original Edition. Milton Keynes: Dauphin Publications.

Power in spending gives you just that the freedom to have options and to enjoy the finer things in life. For most of us to gain that freedom, you may have to sacrifice a few things, change a few habits, and learn to prioritise. You also have to have boundaries for a few years or even a decade to mend the broken legacy and gain a fulfilled legacy to live a good life for both ourselves and the next generation to come.

A perfect example of having freedom of choice is the time when a friend of mine decided to resign from her job. I was shocked that a person could walk away from their role, even when they were good at it.

I asked her why she had made such a drastic move. She told me she did not like being micromanaged and added that she was in the position to resign. Her mortgage was paid for and she had the capital to invest in property along with other offers that were lined up for her.

This is what I would call having the freedom of choice – it should be available for all of us.

If you are not there yet, then you have to create it, and this means gaining control of your spending power.

You want the freedom to be able to buy the finer things in life and enjoy life to the fullest whenever possible, but before you can do that, you have to learn to prioritise things that you want for now and things that you need to help build your future.

Every time you are going to make a purchase, you should ask yourself whether the item you are buying is bringing you closer to freedom of choice or is it holding you back from financial freedom?

Do you want freedom of choice more than the new pair of shoes, outfit, or car?

Or simply say:

- I want freedom of choice more than I want new things!
- I want freedom of choice more than the sweets I am buying from the corner shops!
- I want freedom of choice more than doing my eyelashes and my nails!
- I want this more than my hairstyles that I keep changing every month!
- I want this more than the birthday parties I hold every year!
- I want freedom of choice so that I can fly like an eagle until the end of time!
- I want freedom of choice so that I can buy finer things in life without ever having any regrets!
- I want freedom of choice so that I can live my life's purpose!
- I want freedom of choice for my wellbeing!
- I want freedom of choice so that I never have to compromise myself and allow myself to be bullied!

Write down the affirmation: *I want freedom of choice more than getting* _____. This could be anything you want to purchase out of your spending budget. This should help you prioritise your spending.

Now that you know that freedom of choice is what you would like to have, let it be your aim when you spend your money.

We are constantly hearing that money is the root of all evil. My friend who left her work clearly showed me that money was not the root to evil but a sure path to freedom of choice. What we should be saying is that the mismanagement of money is the root of all evil.

Empowerment in spending allows us not only to learn to spend wisely but to spend with intention and to be clear on what our values are. Once we are clear on those values, then how we spend our money should not be a problem.

Money in this world is a root and a resource to freedom of choice and the sooner you plant that seed in your mind, the faster you can work on entangling yourself from the weeds and start building a legacy.

The fact is that you are free to spend on whatever you want.

You are free to spend

No one can tell you what you should spend your money on, you have the free will to buy whatever you want in life and the only limitation is the amount of money you have in your pockets.

If you want to spend your money on a night out with friends at the end of the month and buy matching outfits from Gucci or Dolce Gabbana so that you look super trendy, then you can. If you want to go on holiday to Ibiza or Miami, then you are free to do so as long as you can afford it.

It pays to be money wise

When you do not have boundaries or limits on your money or any restrictions, you will start living pay cheque to pay cheque. This can cause anxiety, stress, depression, frustration and mood swings and you can also limit your freedom of choice.

Your relationships with others suffer because you are too afraid to admit that you have an issue. You lose out on the things you want like luxury holidays, cruises or being in a position to buy a home, a nice car, and to have a peaceful life.

When I was in my 20s, I worked in Topshop in Oxford Street and at the end of each month, we went to the nearest pub, treating ourselves to a night out. It was almost like a ritual. After all, it was payday and we celebrated with the money we had earned that month.

A few days after the celebration, I soon noticed that I had spent my money rapidly. I had to earn it back the following month. I was forever playing catch up. This was the beginning of me being in the rat race.

I ended up living pay cheque to pay cheque and the process repeated itself like a bad habit. Have you ever heard of a saying that if you keep doing the same thing repeatedly and expect a change, then it's a clear sign of madness? I was walking around with false confidence.

If your dreams and wishes are not big enough, you would end up working for nothing. You are likely to mismanage your money without a single thought in mind, about what is going to happen to you in the following months, years and even decades.

I studied law at Bedfordshire University and in the first two years I had a friend, let's call him Raymond. He was so bright, and he often gave me points on how I should structure my essays. We often revised together in groups.

On most nights, Raymond went out with his friends and he also spent his money on great outfits. During the summer, they often went on holiday and had the latest technology gadgets. By the end of the second year, Raymond dropped out of university because he had accumulated mountains of debt and his parents were unable to bail him out of the financial hole he had created.

I was fortunate to come out with a 2:1 in my degree, but I was saddened that my friend did not complete the course with me. This was not because he lacked intelligence, but merely because he mismanaged his money.

If you had asked me how I spent my money, I would tell you that I had the latest phone, my nails were on point and my hair was always amazing. I also took driving lessons to add to the extra expenses. I went into university with no money, and I came out with debts and student loans. I kept my head above the water.

However, I did prioritise my studies over going out and buying expensive outfits, as well as eating out. Most of my cash was used on purchasing law books, but this was because I have a love for books. I was lucky that my obsession supported my studies, and I scraped through - many students don't.

The last time I spoke to Raymond, he hung up on me and refused to answer my calls. I never saw him again.

After I had finished University, my bank started calling me asking me, when was I going to pay back the money. I was hounded almost every week, which led me to scraping for change. The job offers were not coming in at all. Reality soon hit me, nobody was hiring without experience, and I needed money to pay back the loans. I even sat down wishing I had the guts to be an escort. Luckily for me, I was a size 12 and they wanted girls that were size 10.

Spending freely on presents

We often love to spend on giving our families, friends and acquaintances extravagant presents with money we do not have on occasions such as birthdays and Christmas.

You work so hard trying to make that person or child happy or to show your gratitude - you might even go the extra mile of borrowing the money from family, friends, banks or even loan sharks.

You may often justify this by saying that it's only once in a lifetime and that you will pay it back. The truth is, not even Mystic Meg can predict the future.

I can tell you that in my experience, a day of making someone else happy can bring you a lifetime of misery. After the party, you have to find the money to pay back the loans and also continue paying your bills.

When do you stop punishing your poor soul and give only what you can? If you ask your relatives or friends what gifts you gave them two years ago, they will struggle to remember. People usually remember the time you spend with them and unfortunately, not the gifts.

Maintenance cost

If you are single and dating, do you often wonder where you are going to get the money to keep up with the expensive maintenance of the hairstyles; the nails; the waxing and the perfumes? Not to mention the outfits that must be different every night out with the significant other?

Tell me if you can relate to this: when I started dating my boyfriend, the first joke I told him was that dating was so expensive and that I didn't think I could afford it. He laughed at me (he is still laughing), but I was serious. To make it worse, he worked in a club and often invited me. As much as I love dancing and listening to music, I felt the constant pressure of having to show up.

When he couldn't work in the club for whatever reason, between you and me, I was a bit relieved, because I didn't like the idea of spending to keep up with an image I could not afford.

Everyone loves looking good and it's a great feeling, but it is a temporary feel-good factor. If you do not have the income to maintain it, then it becomes an issue which can cause you depression and lead to long-term mental health issues.

Keeping up with the Joneses (or the Kardashians), is what most of us are trying to do a lot of the time. We do it because we want to fit in, be noticed, liked, approved, and accepted amongst our colleagues, peers, friends, and family members.

We buy perfectionism. The joke is on us when we see a woman without makeup or who has a simple hair do. No nail extensions, no trendy outfits that cost an arm and a leg, happily walking hand in hand with Mr handsome. Then we wonder what happened to perfectionism.

Wealthy people who have limits on their spending, do not give a toss about being approved or accepted by material wealth because they know that if they wanted to buy that Gucci outfit, they could get it. I heard that Warren Buffet still does not drive an expensive car and he still lives in the first home he bought. Whilst some of us might be constantly upgrading every time we get money coming in.

When you are comfortable with the amount of money you have in your pocket, your concerns will be mainly on major issues such as world hunger, social injustice, and world peace.

Your mindset will shift and your perspective on life will change. You will then be able to see the bigger picture and start caring about what matters, not what people think of you.

> ❝ *Everyone loves looking good and it's a great feeling, but it is a temporary feel-good factor.*

How do you spend on the finer things in life?

The rich buy assets that generate income to buy the finer things in life. Therefore, you have to redirect your money to buy tangible assets. This is one of the lessons we should be taught at school or home. This is the trick, this is the golden nugget, the secret sauce. This is the core foundation of becoming seriously wealthy and of course, being able to maintain those assets is also equally essential.

The rich buy assets

If you want to join the list of the richest people in the world, you must buy assets, assets that do not depreciate. Items or services that you can leverage and earn money.

Examples of assets are things like land; properties; vending machines and long-term investments. It may even include starting businesses that solve problems and meet a clear need in your community. Assets such as properties and land can generate revenue, even in times of a recession.

You can rent properties out and gain extra income for yourself, which you can use to save or invest to make even more money.

Most cars do not grow in value, however, if you use the vehicle for delivering goods and providing services then you would have turned a depreciating asset into one that serves you well.

Depreciation means that the price of the item goes down. For example, a car you bought for £5,000, may go down to £2,000 in a few years' time. This means that when you sell it, you will get less money than the price you bought it for in the first place.

The goal should be to buy assets that can make you money or assets that go up in value. A perfect example of this is playing the monopoly game.

The person with more cash and assets wins the game.

To demonstrate the power of buying an asset is the time when my neighbours bought their home for £160,000 - a few years later they sold the house for around £370,000. They made £210,000 back in cash. That's what I call being in the money.

Why buying assets is so pivotal

I spoke to an elderly lady who was celebrating her 87th birthday. She was semi-retired, and I asked her for the best advice she could give us.

She said that we must buy two homes, one to live in and another one to rent out. She also said that having a pension was not enough to live on.

In the book *Rich Dad Poor Dad* written by Robert Kiyosaki, Robert talks about how his wife bought assets that generated an income, so that she was able to spend her money on the car she wanted.

This is the secret sauce that you need to know. To buy the finer things in life, you have to have passive income streams that will support the lifestyle you want.

Even when you're generating all this income, you still need to spend wisely and if you ever need to ask the good

Lord for anything in life, one of your requests should be to ask Him for wisdom on how to make the right choices with the resources He has given you. The right choices will lead you to freedom.

Empower in spending ~ the rich aim for quality, not quantity

Cheap does not always mean it's good; I have learnt this lesson on several occasions.

Have you ever bought clothes from a shop, wore the outfit once or twice, put it in the washing machine, and never been able to wear it again?

I once bought a few bras from a particular shop, and I was so happy about the bargain prices. The bras looked nice and pretty, but I wore them once however, the seams and wiring kept on coming off. I felt like I had just flushed my money down the toilet. I seriously think twice now before buying anything from that shop.

I then bought bras that cost £35 each and they have lasted for ten years. The colour and fitting remained the same and I cannot forget the store that I bought them in.

Whilst dating my boyfriend, I also bought a few jackets from a particular shop, and I aimed to wear different jackets for the night out (trying to keep up with the trend). Each jacket was under £40 (a bargain I thought), but the jackets did not even last the season.

They were not warm enough for the weather, the buttons kept on flying off and the material kept on shredding. This was highly distressing. I was better off putting the £80 together and buying a warm jacket that would have lasted me at least two months of winter, or at least a few years.

The reason why some people go to Marks and Spencer for knickers, is because they sell great quality underwear and clothes. It's the exact reason why people go to Waitrose rather than certain shops for food - Waitrose focuses on quality.

Good quality food will keep you healthy and poor quality food will give you all sorts of diseases. You will end up spending most of your cash trying to reverse the damage you have done to your body over the years.

If you pay attention, you might discover that you may end up paying even more money on items or things that you tried to cut costs on. One jacket that lasts ten years and does the job, is better than a dozen that do not even keep you warm. I am still mad about the jackets.

Go vintage, why not?

Vintage is simply second-hand clothes that are found in charity shops or shops that call themselves vintage. Famous people wear vintage clothes all the time as they cost less, and most are durable. Pride will get us nowhere; smart buying will allow you to keep more of your money so that you can buy assets that help you generate more money.

It does not have to be new to be useful, used and appreciated. If you're buying stuff that is only going to last for a few months such as baby clothes and toys, try and get it for free or exchange clothes with family and friends. Hand-me-downs are great for siblings.

It would be best for you to save the rest of your money or spend it on getting wisdom or buying income-generating assets. A lot of wealthy people get items for free to promote them. For example, you would probably give your t-shirt to Beyonce for free in the hope that she wore it. When her fans see her in it, they are likely to purchase it. The more money you have does not mean the more you should or will spend. It's the opposite and this is one of the reasons why the rich get richer, and the poor remain, just that, poor.

I often found that my friends that were seriously wealthy would direct me to local charity shops where I could find cheaper alternatives, buy it, wear it and then give it back. They felt no way about it, whilst my low-income friends would frown upon me entertaining the thought of entering a charity shop. Your mindset has to change for you to elevate to another level and become seriously wealthy. Or until you can get to the level, where you can get the things you really want in life.

Most of my children's clothes were either second-hand or hand-me-downs because my children were growing out of them every three months. I figured that paying for the mortgage and leaving them a legacy was more important than paying for clothes that only lasted a few months.

Emotional spending - the psychology of spending

Have you ever contemplated running away from home when you were in your teens, for example, as soon as your parents or caregiver said something you didn't like? I have been there, done that. I packed my bags and threatened to leave the family home to avoid those awkward moments in my teens and as a young adult.

During those moments, I visited friends who were not good for me and if they were not available, I went to the corner shops and bought magazines and sweets with the little money I had.

On one occasion, I stopped threatening to leave and took that leap of faith. In that moment, the pain of not being heard, understood, and feeling frustrated with the daily silly arguments with my parents and siblings led me to pack my belongings in black dustbin bags. I finally said those dreaded words: *"I'm moving out."*

I chased freedom. The freedom I was fighting for costed me ten years of loneliness and misery because I was spending on rent, gas, electricity, water bills and council tax. I was never really financially equipped for this responsibility.

On top of the household responsibilities, I had a student overdraft, a maxed-out credit card and a professional studies loan which I took out to go to law school. On top of everything else, I was still trying to impress the silly boyfriends that never had my best interests at all. The banks wanted their money back and there was no job to pay it back.

I lacked financial literacy and I ended up digging myself into a deeper hole. This is what most of us end up doing. We then get stuck in the rat race, chasing freedom, money and work that pays just enough to keep our heads above the water.

I soon learnt a very painful lesson about myself and why I overspent. I learnt how my emotions led me to overspend and I hope that as a reader you will be able to see your patterns in spending too. The sooner you learn from your mistakes, the quicker you can get up and try again.

Financial statements can tell you a lot about yourself. In 2016, I attended a stewardship course at City Gates Church. In one of the assignments, we were asked to look at our monthly expenses and create a budget. It felt awkward and uncomfortable, but I tried.

Whilst I was going through my financial statement, I immediately spotted a pattern - my money was coming out of my account around the same time and on the same days each month. Most of the overspending was going on food at lunch time and it was at a specific restaurant.

Although on the outside the amount seemed very small (£4.59 or £5.60), those small amounts were regular, and they soon accumulated to a large chunk after a year. I was spending over £50 a week on lunches easily without thinking. I had to ask myself why.

I soon realised that I craved peace, space, and time and to be with my thoughts without having to answer to anyone.

At home, I was with family non-stop, and then at work, my job involved constantly talking to people. The only hour I had off, was my lunch hour and although I could sit in the car and eat during the summer, I could not do it during winter. So, I paid the price to gain an hour of peace.

My bank statements made me realise that one of my biggest issues when it came to overspending was that I was emotionally using money to give me space. My mental well-being needed it, but I could not afford it.

What does your bank statement say about you and how you're spending your money?

What is causing you to overspend? Have a look at your bank statements starting with three months and then to six months and then yearly. What are the patterns that you are noticing, and can you redirect them? What can you say no to and why? Also, ask yourself if it is at all possible to get the things you crave for without spending your money?

In 2014, I decided to try and save up money to buy a house. This meant saying no to certain things. I redirected where my money was going, not all of it, but most of it. I said no to buying new clothes, no to getting my nails and hair done regularly and no to spending money on food at lunch.

I became intentional about my spending because I had a goal in mind. This was to save up for a deposit to buy a home for myself and my children.

I had to shred the old me and leave some of the old things behind. In the process, I changed my old ways to move up a ladder or two.

I sacrificed my outer peace for more internal peace when I asked my parents for permission to move back home. I had to go back to the beginning to rebuild my foundation with my finances. I was willing to make that sacrifice to better my future, as well as my children's future.

This meant giving up the Housing Association property which many of us waited 10 years to get. I changed my mindset; I wanted a lifestyle change and I wanted to be the winner in the game of life.

What are you willing to sacrifice to make long-term gains?

In 2016, I finally accomplished my dream of buying a home with support from my parents.

I have spent a great deal of money on the property and it has also given me back a great deal of money to support my projects and to achieve my life's purpose. This is to empower others to fulfil their full potential in life, build renewed confidence and live abundantly.

I continued to learn about how my emotions affect my spending. For instance, a few years later I discovered that although I knew I was earning enough, I never kept the money in my bank account for long enough. I knew how to spend it but keeping it was an issue.

I always found reasons to spend the money. Until I met a financial coach who explained to me that this was to do with my past, that I had somehow been programmed to believe that what comes in must come out.

I began the journey of reprogramming myself so that I could keep my income for longer and make more thereafter.

Analyse yourself if possible and seek therapeutic support for any issues around your finances and how you see your money. Fixing that one issue could be the key to turning your fortunes around.

I urge you to look deeply into your spending patterns by analysing your bank statements and other behaviours that cause you to overspend.

A close look at your bank statement will tell you a lot about where you are right now, and where you are heading. Start by making changes and taking action!

If you don't like the picture you are seeing, then you can stop, pause, or even take a break from spending. Reassess your spending habits and make decisions today to either cut out your old habits or stick with them. Either way, you must do what will lead you to financial freedom.

Swiping that card

A majority of us have been conditioned more than ever to buy our products using our bank cards and credit cards to pay for items in the shop.

This means that you are not able to physically see your money coming out of your hands, which makes it much harder for you to predict how much you are spending. Or to have a moment to think or hesitate for a minute on whether or not you need that purchase today; if you can hold on until next pay or just do without.

Not all transactions show up immediately in your bank account, so you must keep a record and be aware of the money in your account that has already been spoken for, before you make any purchases.

I am going to give you an example: one Friday evening, I bought tickets for my daughter's dance show online and it costed £125.

The balance in my account showed that I still had the £125 in my account on top of my actual balance until the following Tuesday morning. Some card transactions are slower than others to show the true value in the account.

It took until Tuesday morning for the transaction to show up in my account. This means that the balance in my account stayed the same from Friday until Tuesday morning. It was leading me to think that I still had the same amount to spend when this of course was far from the truth. I was -£125 and I had to consciously make a mental note of my spending.

In between those days, I may make a further transaction, perhaps decide to get a takeaway meal for dinner on Sunday night. That transaction may not show up until a few working days later.

If you are relying on your account to show the actual balance in your bank account, you may make the mistake of presuming that the amount in the bank account is higher than it actually is.

To make matters even more confusing, the amount is not considering future direct debits or transactions that have been set up to come out automatically on particular days. It means for a majority of us that if we don't keep records of our spending, then:

1. We are likely to spend money faster than we are getting it.
2. We can easily be deceived into thinking that we have more money in our accounts.
3. We can get distracted and not take note of how we are spending money, meaning that we can without any doubt always be in deficit or spend more than we have in our account.

As an illustration, the account may state that you are in credit by £4,000 and £150 is pending, which in itself is confusing. Why not state the total amount available to spend? The pending amount should not be shown because it has already been spent. So, you actually have £3,850 not £4,000.

The reason why most financial experts would state that it is better to use cash is that you can see exactly how much you are spending immediately. This avoids you going into your overdraft and paying high-interest fees.

Bank cards / Contactless payment are used to buy everything because they're convenient and it cuts down on time. The question is: how much are you spending? It's important to find a solution to how you can buy online without overspending.

Wise counsellors are always available, and it pays to listen to them.

The more time I spend with my mother (one of my wise counsellors in secret), the more I get to learn about how she has become the queen of finances in the family home.

She drops gems every now and again without warning and I am going to share some of them.

Gem One - Always have money spare in your accounts equivalent to your earnings to avoid unexpected transactions in case your wages do not come through on time. She suggests aiming for the amount of your monthly income.

Gem Two - Just because you have £5,000 in your account does not mean you have all that money. Especially if you have not considered future transactions that you are not able to see.

Gem Three - If you can get something for free then get it for free.

Gem Four - Lower your bills where possible.

Gem Five - Cook at home no matter what - it saves money.

Gem Six - Do not buy online if it is avoidable.

Gem Seven - Credit cards... only use it to serve you and pay the money back, don't be a slave to credit.

These gems will serve you well and if you put them into action, you can live a prosperous life.

Online purchases - spending power

At the beginning, purchasing items online seems like an amazing idea, as it saves time and it's very convenient (especially when you can get the items the very next day). However, you must be aware that online purchases tap into your emotional side of wanting and needing to feel special.

The fun part is when you get the parcel and you get to open it. It's almost as if you're opening a gift from a dear friend and you get a feeling of excitement. After some time, that excitement soon disappears and you are then left with a void. After some more time, you start to crave that same excitement again and the only way to get it is to buy again.

The problem with online spending is that it can become addictive and you are more likely to buy impulsively, rather than whether you need the item or not.

When my 19-year-old daughter was ordering almost everything online during the Covid-19 pandemic, my mum was furious. She pointed out the fact that this behaviour was addictive and dangerous. She was spot on, although at the outset it looked safer to buy online - it was another bad spending habit that could get you stuck indoors for longer which also plays on your need to feel nice, wanted and appreciated. It removes the void of loneliness but only for that moment.

Fight off impulse purchasing by creating a plan for every penny you have coming in

1. Plan for your purchases ahead by saving for them, even when you have the exact amount in your account to pay for the item.
   For instance, imagine you would like to buy a car and it costs £12,000.
   Then it is wise to create an account in which you can drip feed in a certain amount. It may take you

years or even months to purchase that car. However, it will save you years of hardship and bad credit. If you want to get the car within a specific time, then you have to get another source of income which does not compromise your wellbeing.

I heard that a famous rapper Jay Z, once stated that if you cannot afford to buy an item three times over then you cannot afford it. It's not a bad way of looking at your money. If you put this concept into practice now, it would save you from overspending on the things that you can't afford.

2. Plan for your wants in the future. For instance, say you want your children to attend grammar school in three years. You know that it might take a sum of money to pay for extra tuition classes, then it is wise to put a sum of money away taking this into account. If you're not sure about the amount you should be putting away, then ask the tutors and add an extra 10% because the price might increase.

   I learnt this from my friend who managed to fund his three daughters' educations. He said that he saved up a year in advance before hiring a tutor. In the meantime, he trained the girls at home, until the time came to pay for a tutor. His only concern was ensuring that they were doing the work. It was not about the cash he was spending to get the extra tuition.

   When I took my first daughter to tuition classes (she was 9 years old at the time), I was counting all my pennies and praying to God that I could make it until the end. My stomach was in knots. If I knew this trick, it would have saved me the worry. She went on to study in a great school, but she had very little chance of getting into Grammar School, because I was financially unprepared at the time for the cost of the tuition and extra learning she needed to prepare for the tests.

> 66 *The earlier you plan for situations, the more likely you are to meet the set goal and achieve your dreams of buying the finer things in life.*

Planning ahead is the key to a balanced mindset

If you plan to go on holiday in two years, then divide the cost of that holiday by 24 months and start putting a monthly sum away each month. It would be almost as if you are entering into a contract with yourself instead of a subscription.

For example, if a trip to Disneyland Paris cost £1500, you divide that by 24 months, which is equal to £62.50 per month. You open a holiday account and start putting away £62.50.

Preparing ahead also gives you room to deal with daily situations, for example, the rising costs of things or the need for extra cash to pay for unexpected things.

Time well spent on being organised can help you fund the finer things in life

Ruth Soukup has a *Living Well and Spend Less* website, she coaches her community on how to organise a home life. I became a member of one of her coaching programmes and she had us write down a list of 20 foods we loved to eat along with the ingredients of how much they costed.

It made me realise how much we could save on money by being just a bit more organised and thinking ahead about our meals. You can even work out when the items you use regularly go on sale in the shops so that you can buy them in bulk, especially things like toothpaste and shower gels. A friend of mine once told me that she preferred to go shopping in the evenings for food because most foods go on sale at that time. She had plenty of money but prioritised how she spent it. If she could get the same things cheaper, then why not?

Being organised and planning ahead is vital for financial wealth and wellbeing. Even if you do that one thing such as plan your food spending for the month, this is one step closer to having control over your expenditure. If you teach the process to the next generation, the legacy will also live on.

Budgets: empower in spending

You can find several spreadsheets online that have budget sheets for you to use and in the past, I have used the Money Saving Expert budget planner. I used it to complete the budget, but I never used it again because it did not take into consideration that my spending fluctuated periodically depending on my situation at a particular time.

I used my bank statement to help me predict some of my expenses, but I could not recall things like the random dentist appointment or any future payments that I had incurred due to taking on a new project.

If budgets work for you, by all means use them. I felt as though they worked to a certain degree because they helped me identify the major expenses such as rent and council tax but not the small costs such as the trips to the sweet shops or the takeaway that I had when I was filling in the budget sheet.

If you are a wiz at spreadsheets and you can walk around with one on your phone, then having a budget might make sense to you.

I do believe writing things down as you spend can be a helpful tool, but you have to be disciplined and be very intentional. A new habit takes time to conquer.

I once had a client who wrote down everything she spent her money on. She wrote this on a piece of paper and told me that it made her realise that she had plenty of money to buy the things she needed. The list helped her become more aware about how her money was spent. She eventually started taking control of her finances by doing that exercise alone.

Budgets are useful if you want a picture of what has occurred with your spending in the last couple of months. They are good at telling you about your history, how much you have spent on things, and it will perhaps allow you to change any unwanted behaviour. However, it's not for everyone and if it's not for you, then be open about it. This will set you free and liberate many people who are not keen on using budgets either.

Young people who are still living at home with their parents or caregivers, should create a superficial budget that reflects where they are now and how much it would be if they moved out of the house. They might even save up before leaving home and add ten per cent more on top of the costs for a much more realistic view. This could be an exercise they could do with their parents every now and again.

So, do budgets really help you save? Do they stop your bad spending habits? Budgets help you see whether you're overspending or whether you need to increase your income. This is a projection of where you are now, but not what you will do tomorrow. Individual expenditures can be unpredictable because there are a lot of factors that we have to consider.

Treat your home like a business when it comes to your finances

Treating your home like a business means having a budget of some kind and going back and forth to make any necessary changes. Remember, this is an ongoing exercise until you have the budget of your dreams or one that suits your needs.

Try looking at your account every day, not every month. If you can create that habit, this will allow more control over your expenses. Telephone banking and banking apps such as Monese are excellent because you will also have your accounts at your fingertips.

If you get into that habit of looking at your account every day, then you will be much clearer on what transactions are coming in and out.

If you treat your home like a business, you will want it to succeed and to always make a profit, not losses. Being the CEO of that business (your home) means that you must manage the company's money and allocate it accordingly. A successful company (your home) means that the CEO is also successful.

The best plan for busy people

In his book, *I Will Teach You to Be Rich*, Ramit Sethi, created *The La Carte Method.*'[15] This system is designed to focus on what you are spending on now. You then have to look at your expenditure and see whether you need it or you want it, and whether you can get it cheaper elsewhere, so that you get good value for your money.

It is a great system, because at times, you end up paying for things you do not need or spend far too much money on items, that you can get at a discounted price when you are able to get the same value at a discounted price.

15 R Sethi, 2020. *I Will Teach You To Be Rich*. 2nd Edition. London: Yellow Kite

The purpose of creating this system is so that you can take note of your money and separate it from the things you love and the things you are just using.

You can empower yourself even further in your spending, by following Ramit Sethi's solution called the *Conscious Spending Plan*[16]. He explains that the *Conscious Spending Plan*[17] allows you to automate your money by putting different amounts into separate accounts. This enables you to take control of how much money you spend and what you spend it on.

His plan is based on young adults who have less responsibility and can therefore adapt to the plan quickly. However, it does not stop you from implementing the plan yourself to fit it in with your lifestyle and then adjusting the percentages accordingly.

In his plan, he splits the amount we spend into three areas:

1. Fixed costs which have to cost around 50-60% of your income
   » Rent
   » Mortgage
   » Loans
   » Gas
   » Electricity
   » Food
   » Clothes

---

16 R Sethi, 2020. *I Will Teach You To Be Rich*. 2nd Edition. London: Yellow Kite
17 R Sethi, 2020. *I Will Teach You To Be Rich*. 2nd Edition. London: Yellow Kite

» Maintenance
» Utilities

2. Investments cost 10% of income
   » Long term investments
   » Short term investments
   » ISA

3. Savings costs 5%-10%
   I have broken this down further, to show you examples of how your savings can be broken down even further than Ramit Sethi's system. It would help if you decided to allocate whatever percentage you are comfortable with.
   » Investment 1% - compound interest
   » Emergency 1% - if you lose your job or income
   » Long-term 1% - buy a house 5-10 years
   » Short term 1% - car breaks down
   » Medium-term 1% - new opportunities - going abroad on holiday - tuition classes
   » Pension 5% - retirement

Guilt-free spending money should be about 20% - 35% such as:

» Spending on yourself
» Money on hobbies
» Money for studying
» Money for birthdays, weddings and other occasions
» Eating out, cinema trips, purchasing books or other spontaneous outings

He then breaks it down as to how each percentage can be split and automatically transferred into different bank accounts so that you're always feeding the other accounts. This will ensure that what is coming in is not always coming out.

In practice, you should look at your bank statement to determine the fixed costs and further expenses. Ramit recommends getting an account that has the highest interest rate. Some online banks pay high interest rates.

If you want to know about the banks that have special interest rates, then go to the Money Saving Expert website, which is updated regularly.

The conscious spending plan is for those who find budgeting difficult and that includes me.

Spending your money on the things you love the most

You are more likely to stick to a plan, method or system, allowing you to spend your money on the things you love the most. Ramit Sethi's *The La Carte Method* enables you to wipe the slate clean, by giving you the grace to stop all your subscriptions and then restarting again and only sticking to the ones you really love.

He said that the system also allows us to see a few things such as:

1. You're probably overpaying already.
2. You're forced to be conscious about your spending.
3. You value what you pay for.

I love the fact that Ramit is taking into consideration the fact that human beings are naturally driven to impulsive purchasing. It is essential to make room for it. If you are an impulsive buyer, then this method should be ideal.

However, there is also the *Latte Factor*[18] which David Bach had introduced to us. The *'Latte factor'*[19] is when you make a list of what you're spending and then cut down on the things that you do not need, such as drinking Starbucks before going to work. David stated that the cost is significant when you add it up.

The Latte Factor is brilliant because it makes you aware of the small holes you create in your purses, that slowly take away your money. The quicker you can patch them up and stop them, the better your finances will be.

For example, buying a sandwich from Pret a Manger and a Starbucks coffee for lunch, can lead you to spend a little over £10 a day. Times that by 5 days and then by 52 weeks and you could have spent over £2600 in a year. I love Pret a Manger sandwiches and hot drinks from Starbucks on occasions, but do I really love it more than going on holiday once a year?

The Conscious Spending Plan is an excellent plan because it allows you to see those small holes you have created in your wallets or bank accounts. You take control of them by

---

18 D Bach, 2004. *The Automatic Millionaire—A Powerful one-step plan to live and finish rich.* London: Penguin Group, p.

19 ibid.

prioritising - buying the things you really love and letting go of those things you don't actually need or desire.

It's a question of:
- Do I need it?
- Why do I need it?
- Does it help me?
- Does it hinder me?

Both authors David Bach and Ramit Sethi agree that automating our money into different accounts is crucial to money management. Whilst David says no to too many lattes, Ramit allows you to spend on the things you love and if it's the latte that makes you complete then so be it. You must love it, so the question remains: what do you love the most?

The power in spending on what we love

One of the things that I discovered about spending on what you love, that makes this concept very significant, is that you can go even deeper and invest your money in educating yourself further. You can also create a business out of those things you love so that you make even more money - this is where passion meets purpose.

For example, I love going to the gym because it makes me feel and look good. I also pay money to use the gym and I decided to complete a gym instructor course so that I can teach people to work out and feel good about themselves. In return for my effort, I would get paid which could then be utilised to pursue my passion even further. Almost like turning the things you love or your passion into profit, so it becomes a win-win.

This is also an example of spending your money on things that can serve you as well as serve others in return for a profit.

Spending on credit cards

A credit card is money that has been given to you on loan. You have to return it within a specific time frame. If you do not return that money, you will incur a fee and interest will be added to the loan you have taken out. If you must use a credit card, you must be able to pay the money back. It also shows other lenders that you can be trusted with borrowing.

A credit card can be used to buy assets so it makes sense to spend wisely. Being good at using credit cards gives you better credit and makes you much more desirable to other lenders. It will also provide you with more access to more credit which you can use to buy assets, such as a house.

Ramit Sethi breaks down how to do this in his book and how to let the credit card work for you. Using direct debits to pay the credit card back on time is also recommended so you do not miss the deadlines.

However, if your spending habits are bad, I would agree with Dave Ramsey and David Bach and would urge you to avoid using credit cards because they could cause more pain than pleasure.

My recommendation for a house rule:

You should only pay for items using credit cards when you have the money to pay them back. Or be prepared to buy on the credit card today, then pay it off the following day or within the time frame because this will stop you from incurring extra charges, which can be extreme from 29.9% or more.

Buying things on our credit cards in the hope that we will receive the money later or in a month to pay it off is like having blind faith. It will cause anxiety and frustration, which you should try to avoid.

Whilst spending on credit cards, you must take into consideration the money that you need to spend next month or the month afterwards that has already been accounted for.

Then what's left over is probably the money you will have left to pay off the credit card.

You cannot predict the future. You can only live in the present and prepare for the future just in case things don't go as planned.

God's money

If all else fails, tap into your faith whenever you are about to spend your money unwisely. A little prayer might be all it takes for you to make the right decision.

I am the type of person who looks after other people's things better than my own. I can look at your finances and spot the holes and areas you need to control so that you can spend more on the finer things in life.

One of the exercises that helped me be a better steward of my own cash and take inventory as to how I spent it, was the fact that I had to acknowledge that it was not my money, but God's money.

I am just a steward, a guardian, and a manager who has to decide how to spend it according to God's needs.

If I manage what He has given me badly, then the likelihood is that He will not give me anymore until I learn to manage it well.

This view gives me an extra layer of protection and control. It helps me say no to overspending, impulse purchasing and unnecessary borrowing. After all, I am managing God's money and I want to be the best manager in his eyes.

Summary

Seven Key Notes

Freedom is having the sense to do what's right for you, bearing in mind your emotions, your capabilities and being okay with having boundaries. It's the same way a driver cannot drive their car more than 70 miles per hour on a 30-mile-per-hour road – it can lead to a fatal accident. This is why it is so crucial to get the correct mindset and also be able to control your emotions and spend well.

Seven Key points in empowering spending.

1. You should take inventory of your past spending habits by going over your bank statements at least once a week or a month.

   Schedule that appointment like it is your doctor's appointment.

   I would suggest you find someone who is non-judgmental and whom you trust to go through it with you. Listen to their opinion, even if it hurts, then turn to God for strength for you to make the right decisions.

2. You should follow *The La Carte Method* and start cutting out your subscriptions on all the things that you do not love and things that are not supporting your values. Redirect your cash to those subscriptions that you love and value the most.

3. Complete the *Conscious Spending Plan* and open up the high-interest bank account and savings account, (this may take a few weeks). Once it's done, it's done. If it's causing you a headache to pick the bank with the best interest account then don't worry, open up any account and start drip feeding in that money.

4. Automate your accounts and allocate a percentage to each account each month, start off small and then increase it. This is not a sprint but a marathon - complete at the pace that is comfortable for you.

5. Time to sit back, relax and set a date for a financial review of your spending plan. Have a fixed slot

because you must check in every now and again to make sure that it works.

6. Don't give up - remember the legacy is yours to establish.

7. Focus on buying assets to generate more income by using the automatic system. What is that thing that will make you even more money so that you can increase those percentages? Your focus should be on improving the percentages every quarter, or even better every month.

CHAPTER 3

Empower in Overcoming Money Blocks

> 66 *Money is like blood...money is our economic lifeblood... Money is integrated into all aspects of your life. We need it to help our system function and without it we are not able to function properly.* [20] 99

I f money is like blood, then we should try to ensure that it flows freely in our system.

What happens to blood when it cannot flow freely throughout the body?

I can only guess that the lack of free-flowing blood would create an issue, an area of concern, a problem or something that is blocking the overall functioning of the human body. This issue may not be known but it can cause pain, frustration and it also cripples your wellbeing and any growth.

---

20 Rabbi Lapin, D., 2014. Business Secrets From The Bible- Spiritual Success Strategies For Financial Abundance, New Jersey / Canada: Wiley, p.212

You may try to take painkillers or use a compression every now and again to help reduce the pain. However, sooner or later you must find out the cause of the issue and try to get rid of it or find the right medication to keep it under control.

An unclogged vein will cause stress, anxiety, depression and feelings of inadequacy. You are then left not wanting to do anything and have no choice but to seek medical advice from a doctor or therapist. You may even turn to the Bible, a friend, financial coach, or an empowerment coach.

This is precisely what can happen to you with your money. You may find that the system you created is somehow not flowing properly, leaving you with no money to do the things you would like to do. Perhaps you like getting your nails done or going on holidays. Maybe you want to pay for a course to learn new skills, or to fly in first class, or own a jet, or start your own business.

Before you tackle the money blocks, the first question you should ask yourself is, do you have a system for how you use your money? Are you in control of what is coming in and out?

If not, then you must go back to chapter two and create the system. Without a system you cannot function at all or see the patterns that are causing your money blocks.

Is the system you have created any good? Is it overflowing or is it clogged up?

You know the system is working when you see a flow of money in your named accounts, and you are not constantly digging from one account to feed the other one.

It is essential to review your system (accounts) regularly. Set yourself a set time and date for examining them. For example, every Wednesday after 7pm, I will do an audit on my accounts.

When I took my driving test, one of the things I had to do was take a hazard perception test. Before I took the test, I prepared for it, this meant practising the exercises.

I recall one exercise that I had to deal with, when my car was driving in the road and all of a sudden, a ball came dashing into the middle of the road, (or on some occasions a pedestrian would try to cross the road). I would have to spot the hazard quickly enough to avoid an accident. Although this made my car stop or slow down, it was inevitable that I had to act.

Now let's compare it to having money. You may not have been taught how to spot the hazards that could either stop your money from flowing freely in and out of the system, or ones that are bound to block your system resulting in it not working.

The consequences of those unlearnt lessons means that you are more likely to be taken by surprise, shocked or unprepared for those hazards that potentially could stop your money from growing and prospering. It could also stop you from walking in your purpose and fulfilling your true potential in life.

Once you recognise the problem and have seen the effects it has on you and your family, you may start looking for solutions, ideas to help you deal with these blocks that are stopping you from excelling.

You would know that you have dealt with the money block because you would have an increase in empowerment, renewed confidence, and abundance. You would be happy.

In this chapter, I will look at the several areas in your life that can cause money blocks such as education or the lack of it, as well as your personal relationship with money and with others.

What you perceive as wealth, the misconceptions that can drive you towards specific behaviour trends and your environment, may be why you are not growing in wealth and why you may have significant money blocks hindering your growth.

What is your relationship with money?

In the last chapter, one of the things that I talked about was the time when I discovered that I had a mindset that told me what comes in, must come out. It made me think about my own personal relationship with money.

Where did that very thought come from?

I had to go back in time and ask myself what my first encounter with money was. What role has it played in my life and how do I see with it?

How could I unblock this thinking process so that I could keep more money in my pocket and live the life that I truly deserve?

This is precisely what I would like you to do either in groups or on your own. Go back to where it all began so that you can understand the cause of your money blocks and find a solution that will lead to a better personal relationship with your money.

When I was about 11 years old, my mother gave me a piggy bank and she also helped me open up a bank account in my name. I do not recall her telling me "*Sandra you must save all your money*," but I assumed that this is what I had to do with any money I received. I therefore saved any change that I got from my dinner money. I saved that money because the chips in school costed 40 pence and I also had a small drink. Any change left from the dinner money went straight into the piggy bank.

One morning, my elder sister found money in my piggy bank. She ran to tell my father that I had a lot of money. He then reduced my dinner money to 50 pence instead of £1 at that time. He obviously did not consider inflation.

I could not save any more money, because I had just enough to spend on my school dinners. I finally found the courage to let him know that the school dinner money had gone up and I therefore needed the increase. I never saved up any money again after that punishment.

I had my first job at the age of 14 delivering cable books my aim was to have some pocket money. When I worked in my second job at Boots, I spent my first wages on buying a Panasonic music station and some music CDs.

I then met an Irish friend of mine called Libby. She helped me get my third job working at Homebase. We often walked at least five miles to go to work and I noticed that she had biscuits for lunch to save money. So I began to mimic her, until my mother saw me walking to work and she asked me, what was the point of earning money if I couldn't afford to get the bus to work.

I stopped walking from home, which was from Tower Hamlets all the way to Leyton. After all, I was working. What good was money if I could not spend it?

This is where my journey with spending money recklessly began. From then and even beyond my university years, I spent money like it was a water stream coming down freely.

I had no intention or mind set to save it, because I had no vision for its future and what it could do for me. I never felt poor or rich because I had student loans and a part-time job that took care of my immediate needs. I knew I had to work for it because both my parents went to work. I thought this would be forever.

The stream dried up at some points and even then, I did not take note that I had to save my money. I just thought I have to get a job and I would be just fine.

The thought of saving money became my priority when I was bullied at work for the second time. I finally asked myself what it was that was causing me to feel so much pain, because the truth is nobody loves their job that much to endure pain from another human being. Unfortunately, I had to due to lack of money management skills and money blocks.

What about you? Write out in your journal your very first encounter with money and read it back to yourself to discover your money blocks. You may discover the lies and the truth that you have been taught about money and how it is potentially hindering your progress. Then begin to rewrite your own story about money.

The rewritten story should be about how great you are now with money and the life you are living now; that you have created an abundance of it and you now have the knowledge to manage it properly. You are now living the life you want, living within your means and are focused on fulfilling your full potential in life. There is no lack of money or wisdom. You are now saving more money whilst growing and spending your money wisely. You will see your mind starting to change and your thoughts becoming rewired.

To unclog the negative relationship you may have with money, you can also seek counselling or a therapist to begin to form a new relationship.

66 *Our thoughts are the consequences of our environments*

Being in a different environment, exposes us to either want more than what we have, or to want less. After all, if your eyes have not seen it and your ears have not heard about it, why should you dream of wanting it?

When I lived in Tower Hamlets, most of my acquaintances and friends lived in council properties. All I heard was how difficult it was to get a council property and how we had to be on the waiting list for at least 10 years before you could be offered a council flat.

Nobody ever spoke about buying a house or even renting, so my thoughts were on how I could get on the council list and not on how to buy a house. The mere fact that I could spend those years saving for a deposit for a home did not even occur to me. My thoughts were led by my surroundings. Are your thoughts led by your surroundings and are you thinking small, when in fact you can think bigger than where you are right now?

For my mind to change, I had to move away from that environment. My attitude shifted from wanting to be in a council flat, to wanting to be a homeowner.

It took stepping away from my environment to want more for myself. In fact, even when my parents bought their flat, my mind still remained the same, until I let go of the old friends and made new friends that spoke the same language but had different thoughts. They spoke of owning homes, saving, holidays and businesses. So, I began to think that same way.

Education vs. Money

The lies you are told and those that you constantly tell yourself are that:

Education is the only key to wealth. I used to think that having a good education, being a good student and getting good grades is all I had to do to become a success story. With success, a great job with money follows and I thought I could build wealth from just being a good student.

Instead of aiming for my dancing and singing career (which was what I was naturally good at and writing poems and songs), I went to study law because it seemed like a clear path to success. After all, I loved reading and defending people. I was never pushed into a particular type of career from my parents - they knew I had talent in dancing and music and they nurtured it by paying for my lessons when they could afford it.

If I said I wanted to be a doctor, they would have said supported that too. At the time, I never felt any pressure to be something I was not. It's only when I stepped into the world of work, that I started to feel limited and somehow limited from becoming more. I felt the iron gates closing in on me, but I could not put my fingers on why I felt like this. I would make numerous applications and get nowhere. Internally, I started to feel as though there was something wrong with me, that I was not good enough.

I spent a lot of money on education and paying £8,500 for law school seemed logical to me as the plan was to earn at least £60,000 a year.

You can get disappointed at times, when you realise that education is just a foundation block for knowledge which can be used in all aspects of life. Some might succeed on that path and others may not. Those that do not make it may have a sense of failure. Why not me? The truth is it may never have been your path in the first place. Just because you can do something, doesn't mean it's your calling.

When people ask me why I am not pursuing a law career, I used to say things like I had to look after my daughter as an excuse. The truth is, this may have never been my purpose. God most likely knew that I could help and serve people in other ways and use my knowledge to support others, whom I would have never encountered if I had become a lawyer.

I fed people the lie they wanted to hear when the truth was that law was never really my passion. It was a goal that I pursued for status and for money, hence why it was easy for me to give up on. It was never my true passion or what I truly wanted to do.

You must have a clear vision of where you are heading. Without it, you are heading nowhere.

This belief that education is a path to success (which is clearly a lie), has stemmed into my adult life and I have manifested it into my children's lives. It was no surprise that when my child turned two and half, I enrolled her onto the Kumon tuition programme.

My attitude was that the earlier she learns basic Maths and English, the greater chance of success she will have. I wanted her to do better and be better than myself. The honest truth is, I prioritised education amongst other things as a key to a more excellent path. I know the truth, because I have seen it with my own eyes that even those who are illiterate, can actually become successful even beyond our expectations.

For example, a friend of mine dated a mechanic who knew all things about cars and could fix them quickly, but he lacked literacy skills. She knew this because she would read his letters for him. I may be literate, but I certainly cannot fix cars. The trick is to work within your own ability. When you do that, anything is possible.

I am not saying that education does not bring you success, as it is a pool of knowledge that can help us improve our lives, in the hope of improving other people's lives. However, it does not determine how successful you will become.

When you hear that people like Richard Branson and John Major never passed their A-Levels and still became successful, then that should assure you that financial success is not about education. It is more about your life skills, your mindset and your environment.

> ❝ *True riches are mainly built on what you actually love to do to serve your community rather than how many degrees or certifications you have.*

One of the life skills you should invest in is financial literacy, no matter what path you take. This can help you build a firm foundation for your life and as a result, you can have freedom of choice rather than become trapped in toxic environments, that would eventually lead you to unhealthy lifestyles and low self-esteem.

Having a great job

I used to think that having a great job that paid well was a key to success - more money, better life. However, when I experienced bullying at work on many occasions, it actually made me overspend my money as a coping mechanism. I started spending my money on things that promised me a better life at the other end. I began to look for a way out, and that meant paying for more courses without a clear direction and burning even more money in the pursuit of happiness.

I wanted out instead of getting internal support, like a Union representative or speaking to my GP. People often forget that when you're being hurt, you don't know who to turn to for support. Sometimes our minds can even tell us that they are all in on it and that they won't provide any help.

When people get bullied or mistreated, it doesn't just affect your well-being. It also affects how you deal with your resources and your relationships with others. People could only see the tears in my eyes but not how broken I was becoming.

They did not see what it was doing to my finances, my spirit and my soul as a human being. It breaks you as a whole. I had come to realise that whilst you are being bullied, you can make illogical decisions like gambling in the hope that you will one day hit the jackpot. However, in reality, you are losing a lot of your money.

So, instead of saving my money to get freedom, I was spending it excessively which resulted in me trapping myself even more. I had to learn to seek help from the right people and therapy to help me deal with the trauma inflicted upon me.

You can have a great job that pays you well above six figures. Whether you are an entrepreneur or employee, it is so important to put money aside for a rainy day. That money can be used to support yourself and empower you to leave your role and find other opportunities. Or it might help you gain a sense of confidence that no matter what happens at work, you're going to be just fine. It can also be used to defend yourself, if required.

A friend once said to me that I should make sure I had £3000 in my account, just in case I need to go to the tribunal. Although he said it in jest, he was right. Legal aid for employment disputes may not be available for you, so you may need that extra cash to fight your employer against any wrongdoing. In fact, you may need even more money for therapy to recover from your brokenness and repair any trauma and learn how to cope with it afterwards.

Having more money or earning more does not mean that you will be happy. It should not be surprising to hear that rich, famous people are committing suicide such as: Robin Williams who was alleged to have committed suicide in 2014; Cheslie Kryst in 2022 (she was Miss USA 2019) and Caroline Flack, British TV presenter who committed suicide on 15th February 2020. Having money does not exempt you from having problems.

You can sometimes be able to predict that you have underlying issues even when your income is sufficient. When you suddenly start overspending, buying stuff to please others or to make yourself feel good. When you are still holding on to old wounds or feel inadequate for some reason. When you are too concerned about meeting society's expectations of being married and having children.

One of the lies I used to tell myself was that I must have a man to become successful.

This lie stemmed from reading news reports about single parents and how much support they needed. In fact, I thought being a single parent meant living a life of poverty, which was clearly not true.

I tried not to become that single parent, so I dated men and often tried to make them conform to this idea that we should be a united front. However, they were only thinking about getting 'that thing.' Coming from a home which had both parents only made me consolidate my belief that being a single parent would lead to an unsuccessful life.

After finishing law school, I became a parent via Special Guardianship Order. At that time, she was five years old. I became a single mum from then on. I had to learn a few things quickly like, I could not go out at midnight to buy onions because I had a little one to take care of.

As a single mother working full time, I was surrounded with co-workers that were married. They often spoke to me about the houses they had with their spouses and where they were going on holidays.

So, I thought that all I needed to do was find that good man to settle with, so that I too could have financial freedom to be able to buy a home and go on these fancy holidays. The truth of the matter was that I had plenty of money to be able to do those things with my child. We were a family and still are a family with or without a partner in my life. It took me going through the motions to note this fact.

I finally found my prince

On a cold November day in the shopping centre, I bumped into a guy I once fancied in secondary school. I thought this was it and that God has finally answered my prayers. He was still attractive and after a few conversations, we started dating.

A few months into the relationship, I asked him to help me with my personal training assessment by acting as the person who I was training.

Whilst in the waiting area, we met a lady who I started up a conversation with about having a pension and buying a home and the lady had persisted in saying that she believed that buying a house was better than having a pension.

I told her that it was not possible for a single parent to buy a house on her own. She replied that this was not true and she herself was a single parent. She was actually doing it on her own with two children and she had a second home now.

I became even more curious, so I asked her, *"How do you manage? What if you were fired from your job?"* The lady responded that at one point she was made redundant from her job. She then decided to get a lodger to help pay for the mortgage whilst she shared a room with her children, until she found another job. She told me that *"you just do what it takes."*

After six months of dating this prince, I asked him whether we could raise money and buy a home together and he replied: *"You can do this on your own."*

That comment alone made me realise that he was not my prince charming and as you can imagine, our relationship never lasted that long.

I realised that waiting for 'Mr right' to start my journey was a waste of time so I began to think of ideas and ways I could raise the deposit on my own. In 2016, I got my keys to my first home, although, I was a single parent with two children.

I got support along the way from my parents, but I would have never done it, if I was stuck in that mindset of being a single parent meaning I was not able to do certain things. In fact, I now say that we all have the resources to fulfil our full potential in life and you must start with what you have right now.

Being alone does not mean you are unable to do things, it just means that you must think a little differently from the norm and plan to pursue your goals and dreams. If I never met that woman at that course, I would still be searching for prince charming to buy a home with. That fairy tale story we have been told time and time again is not reality and realising that it is just that (a fairy tale) is a sign of maturity.

Relationships ~ how they can block your money from growing and how you can overcome and build an empire together

Data released Wednesday by financial firm TD Ameritrade found that 41% of divorced Gen Xers and 29% of Boomers say they ended their marriage due to disagreements about money.[21]

Dr Myles Munroe has stated '*Whatever you give a woman she is going to multiply it.*'[22]

He argues that when a woman gets money from her husband, he must trust and believe that she will do something with the money which will multiply the amount. Most men are so afraid of giving their money away to a woman that in most cases they end up broke, or when a woman is not receiving any cash from a man or ideas to build their empire, the relationship dwindles and the cash flow becomes blocked causing a strain on the relationship.

In some cases, if a man is not financially stable, it could be because he is dividing his money between multiple families that he has created or co-relationships with other women which he cannot afford to maintain. If he is always without money but busy working or is not able to bring dough in

21 Catey Hill, 2018. Moneyish. [online] Available at: *marketwatch.com/story/this-common-behavior-is-the-no-1-predictor-of-whether-youll-get-divorced-2018-01-10* [Accessed 26 Nov 2022]

22 Dr. M, Munroe, 2018. Understanding The Purpose And Power Of Women: God's Design for Female Identity, Expanded Edition with study guide, Nassau, Bahamas United States: Whitaker House

the house, you must ask yourself one question: who else is in your relationship?

One of the lies that are installed in men is that most women are gold diggers. This stems yet again from media stories when they talk about divorce settlements and how much the woman has received, without breaking down what the woman has had to do to support the man throughout the years. Songs like *Gold Digger* by Kanye West only perpetuate the stereotypes.

There are men and women out there in society who are only after another person's money - it would be very naive of us to think that it is just women.

Some women have been brainwashed into believing that they are princesses, and that prince charming is coming to rescue them – they also believe he must be wealthy. Look at Cinderella and Sleeping Beauty. The truth is no one is rescuing anyone, it's teamwork.

Teamwork builds an empire

When both men and women realise their true potential, they compliment each other. He thinks of the idea, and she will help him plan it out and they can both execute it or vice versa. The entire family will gain from the fortune.

However, if one is not sharing ideas, fails to communicate them to the other person at home and strives to accomplish everything on their own, the empire will never be built. Both individuals will find themselves trapped in an unhealthy relationship which is unsustainable and very unproductive.

Somebody will always be complaining about something, which is more than likely going to be money related.

I know a woman, who worked so hard for her partner and children - she paid most of the bills in the house. He was always away for business. She never stopped to question why he never had any money. She was so in love with the idea of having a husband and forgot about the doubts she had in her head, his constant absence, and the fact that the businesses were never profitable.

The issue came to light when the bailiffs came to repossess their property, because her husband had borrowed £35,000 on the house. Although he was given warning letters, he ignored them, so the £35,000 bill turned into £85,000.

The couple had to sell the property and this was when they decided to separate. She was left with no home, a bad credit report and a broken heart. The fact is that the evidence was there, but she chose to ignore it because she was so in love with the idea of having a husband, rather than what a good husband should do to keep the family home.

From my own experience, I've seen that couples can be lonely in their relationships. You can easily become single parents within the relationship if you find yourself doing all the hard work. Paying for a majority of things, as well as taking care of the children. My guess is that you are a single parent in disguise.

When a couple work well together, they can overcome any crisis. One of my colleagues Beatrice and her husband worked super well together. When he was made redundant from his job which caused him a great deal of anxiety, he was able to focus on finding another job. She had also saved up £20,000 and that money was used to pay the mortgage until he found another job.

Do you think their love for each other grew stronger or was it weakened by the crisis?

They had to adjust and cut down on their expenses, which she understood was difficult for him because he loved the finer things in life. He eventually found a better job that paid him even more money. She later told me that she treated her home like a business and that she was responsible for the family's finances.

If this happened to you and your partner today, would you be okay because of money you have saved up?

The bottom line is as a couple, you should be at a point where you can discuss money coming into the household and money coming out freely. Is there a plan to build on what you have or don't have? Are you elevating each other financially or destroying each other? Do you have any money blocks to overcome as a couple? We all come with our own sack of blocks in our relationships and those have to be dealt with to sustain a loving relationship.

Communication is pivotal in relationships and the one thing you should be able to do with your partner is to be open and not judge, because love does not judge.

Love understands that people are unique and see things differently. As one, you and your partner should have a common goal which is to be in a better place financially together, to build a legacy and to have freedom of choice for the family so that you can all enjoy life's treasures.

Without communication in a marriage or in any partnership, you and your significant other might as well be sailing on dry land.

I genuinely believe that if you are in a relationship whereby you are having to hide your money because somebody is not good with money, or you do not trust each other when it comes to money related issues, and are not able to see each other's transactions, this says a lot about your relationship and where it's heading. If you're married, it's probably going to end in divorce, or someone is bound to stray which puts even more strain on the family resources and wellbeing.

The bottom line is that in any relationship, all bank statements must be laid bare. This includes debts and any emotional attachment you and your partner may have over money and spending habits. Then, as a couple you have to be able to draw up a plan that takes into consideration each other's strengths and weaknesses so that you can build an empire. After all, you both want the same thing for yourself and the family – financial freedom and living in your full potential, without any financial setbacks.

Wellbeing, emotions, hormones, and feelings

Human beings have been created to have five senses - we can see, touch, smell, taste and hear. Within us, we have our own biological makeup that triggers our hormones and in return causes us to either spend on things we sometimes do not need.

In the Cosmopolitan article *How Your Cycle Makes You Spend Money in Weird Ways*,[23] it talks about the different things we spend our money on according to our levels of oestrogen and progesterone. This is why at times you may reach out to buy chocolate or make up to make you feel better. You may find yourself grabbing sweets just before or during your menstrual cycle - I certainly do.

In the article *Why do we spend? What science says about our personal finances*, Melissa Leong, wrote that:

> 'Scientists found that people infused with oxytocin donated to 57% more causes and 56% more money than those who were given placebos. Whenever we raised oxytocin, people willingly opened up their wallets and shared money with strangers.'[24]

Seasons and whether it's light or dark, colours, sounds, happy moments, and the feeling of sadness can trigger your emotions and as a result you may take out the credit card, and buy, buy, buy. I used to work for House of Fraser and as I would walk into the store, I felt great because the store was lit so well. The light brightened up the store and as sales advisors, we would put on an extra smile for customers. I am sure that some customers brought items for a hefty

23 *Elizabeth Narins*, 2015: How Your Cycle Makes You Spend Money in Weird Ways [online] Available at: *cosmopolitan.com/health-fitness/a39084/ how-your-cycle-affects-your-shopping-habits* [Accessed 27 Nov 2022]

24 Melissa Leong, 2014: Why do we spend? What science says about our personal finances- *Why do we spend? What, in our brains, leads us to take on bigger mortgages than we can afford? Leading scholars explain our money behaviour* [online] Available at: *financialpost.com/personal-finance/ why-do-we-spend-what-science-says-about-our-personal-finance*

price and signed up for store cards in an instant because they felt good.

It is important to be aware of the fact that your emotions may be the catalyst that is leading you to overspend. Once you can recognise this, you can create systems and barriers to stop you from making purchases that you didn't want to buy in the first place.

It's essential to build a solid group of people who understand that at times, your emotions are leading you to spend - they can remind you that your journey to build and create wealth is vital. Someone cannot stop you from buying unwanted stuff, however, a gentle reminder of the fact that uncontrolled spending may result in you having less freedom to do the things you love, might help you put a limit on your spending habits.

> 66 *Money blocks can stop you from spending on the right things*

You may want everything to be within your price range and also be of good quality but unfortunately, good quality things often come at a price.

If your mindset is always looking for a bargain and are too adamant that you will not pay the full price for that thing you need, you might end up disappointed. Those who offer the cheaper options might have hidden fees which might lead you to pay the full price in the long run or you may not get the full service you requested.

For example, if you decide to go on a diet to lose weight, you may spend a lot of money by taking supplements and shakes. You then spend money on a yearly gym membership, but you are clueless on how to use the equipment effectively. The gym instructor's role is to show you, how to use the equipment once and safely. You don't even know where you are going wrong because you seem to be doing the work and are turning up three to four times a day. However, years have gone by, you are still weighing the same and are not seeing any results.

Your solution could be to hire a personal trainer. Doing this could save you years of overspending and frustration of trying to lose weight at the gym, without seeing results.

I found this out when I got a personal trainer to help me train for a half-marathon. Within six months of training, my body looked amazing and in better shape and I wondered what the heck I had been doing at the gym over the last 10 years.

I never knew how to train correctly and use the gym equipment to get the results I wanted. I was so afraid of paying for a personal trainer because I thought that I could not afford it. The truth was I was wasting more money and time without proper support.

What are you wasting your money on? What is stopping you from paying a premium price and getting the results you actually want?

Families overcome money blocks

The best thing a family can do is to rely on each other for support. A family that works together as one can become unstoppable. The aim is for everyone in the family to prosper.

You are an asset for your family and your family members are also assets. You should be able to tap into each and every member of the family's talents and gifts. When used correctly, you can all win and build an empire. Family disputes and not seeing each other as one can cause money blocks.

One of the keys to removing any family disputes is to start seeing the family as a business. Start seeing yourself as an asset and your children as assets too. Why work for someone else when as a family, you could work together to support each other's dreams?

Let's say for instance, that your dream as a family is to buy a home. Here's an example, Junior 1 and Junior 2 have reached the age of 18 and 21 and their dream is to travel. They are both earning £1000 part time whilst still studying and living at home. Their parent is earning £2,300.

Here is an example of household bills:

BILLS	COST (£)
Rent	1100
Gas and Electric	100
Council Tax (per month)	108.33
Water (per month)	40
Food	200
Travel	120
Clothes	50

If the parent was paying for everything, s/he would have £581.67 left in the account.

If Junior 1 and Junior 2 gave their parents or the parent £400 each (total £800) towards the cost of the house keep, they would each have £600 left to save or use for hobbies, travel, clothes, etc, per month.

The parents or parent could put the £800 towards a deposit for a home. After 10 years, the amount would be £96,000 with interest, if put into an interest savings account.

If they then had a mortgage, they could pay a rate as cheap as £600 a month depending on the mortgage rate they decided to take out. The bigger the deposit, the cheaper the mortgage rate is in most cases.

They would have reduced their rent from £1100 to a mortgage of £600, saving a total of £500 and have an asset that goes up in value most of the time. Yes, they would have more responsibility towards the house like fixing the boiler, but they could get insurance and put some money aside towards new opportunities.

They could also use the £500 to pay towards the mortgage, getting the mortgage down even faster and save the rest towards another property.

If the mortgage has been fully paid for after ten years, the parent(s) or child(ren) would live rent free.

Here's a table when they are mortgage free:

BILLS	COST (£)
Rent	0
Gas and Electric	100
Council Tax (per month)	108.33
Water (per month)	40
Food	200
Travel	120
Clothes	50

The total of all bills is £618.33 (add 20% for inflation) plus £123.666 = £741.996. Rounded up is £742 and then divide the amount between three members of the household - they would pay £ 247.33 per month towards the bills, and they get to keep the rest of their money. This could be the family's reality over a period of 20 years.

The children may have obtained higher-paying jobs by then too. They could then put some money towards another deposit for another home which they could rent out. That could be the rental income which could create passive income and so forth for the family and generations to come.

If you do not look at your family as potential assets and resources to growing your wealth as a well as the entire family's wealth, you could end up with a broken legacy.

When we do not see the bigger picture

A lovely acquaintance of mine found good fortune through her sister who had won the lottery. Her sister gave her money to buy herself a house for the family. Within a few years, she had moved her boyfriend into the house.

The boyfriend took out a loan against the house that was worth £7,000. He then left her for another woman. She felt like she was not able to pay the £7,000 debt on the house and when she asked her children to help her (they were in their 20s), they refused to support her reminding her that it was her fault she was in this situation.

She felt like she had no choice but to sell the house, so that she could pay off the debt. Both mother and daughters had to move out and start renting. As a result, they had lost an asset and ended up increasing their overheads by renting.

Families have their ups and downs. However, within the family unit, you all want one thing and that is freedom of choice. This includes more options in life and to be able to fulfil one's potential without worrying about money. The quicker you can start working towards this as a family, the better future each member of that unit will have for generations to come.

Money blocks within the family, whether extended or immediate, occur when individuals do not see the benefits that everyone brings to the table or how each person can contribute to the household.

When you hear families feuding, it is mostly likely going to be over the little things like wearing clothes, who has left the bathroom untidy, parents not giving space to their children and children not supporting their parents.

Misunderstandings over everyone's mental state or ability can also play a major role. Truth be told, we are all not the same. The potential the families can achieve once all is said and done is tremendous - the family is a business and an empire on its own.

Families can be the biggest helpers or hindrances when it comes to supporting each other in the areas of finances, mindsets and how happy someone is in life.

I live in a multi-cultural community and I have witnessed how families that work together have been able to manage their finances well and avoid money blocks.

One of my Asian friends once told me that in their tradition once they got married, the wife would typically live with the in-laws for a while. This saves money and the couple get support with the children when they are young. By the time they move out, they would have saved for a deposit or be able to buy a house outright. Either way, they would be financially secure.

I did ask him an awkward question which was how they got privacy and time out. He said that they go away for weekend breaks.

In my culture, being a Ugandan living with your in-laws is frowned upon, whilst other cultures see it as a great strategy to save money and get immediate support if you're just starting out as a couple.

I was listening to one of Dr Myles Munroe's YouTube videos on finance. I recall him saying that he had to live with his in-laws when he married his wife and the pressure of not wanting to live there, pushed him to save even more money so that they could buy their first home. He died a multi-millionaire, but he could never have achieved it without that support.

My best advice to a young person contemplating leaving home, is to get your finances in order and become financially literate because freedom comes from within, not from the outside world.

When I left home straight after university, I wanted to have my own space and I was sick and tired of the meaningless bickering and blame games that I encountered time after time. I had student loans that needed to be paid, a maxed-out credit card and a part time job. I also wanted to attend law school which came with a hefty price tag. My emotions and frustration took over so I decided to move out.

After talking to my friends and listening to the dynamics and the benefits of living with family, I had to take a step back and think about whether this was feasible. After speaking to my mum, she agreed that I could move back in the family home. I gave back the keys to my flat and moved in with my parents.

Most of my friends from Caribbean and African backgrounds thought it was a bad move, but others predominantly from the Asian background thought it was a great idea. One guy even said that if I did not buy a house, I could start my own business with the money.

After 10 years of trying to make it on my own, I moved back to my parents' home. I had to start all over again because that was the only way I could raise enough cash for my home and financially support my children. I would be lying if I said it was easy, but it was a necessary sacrifice that would enable me to get closer to freedom.

The move allowed me to start my own business, pay for coaching programmes to improve my business and personal development and to also invest in this book. It's allowed me to be able to fulfil my full potential in life, so that generations after me globally can also reap the rewards from my book and my services.

As I write, prices are going up on almost everything. This is the time for families to rethink and strategise - how are you going to manage so that you can elevate together? A win for one family member is a win for all.

Friends with a common goal

If you do not have immediate families or if you're not surrounded by family, you could try sharing a flat or a rented property with friends who have a common goal. Usually, the bills are lower because you're sharing them and the rent is also lower.

One of my good friends told me that as soon as he turned 16, his mother told him to leave the family home. He shared a house with a few friends and saved most of his money. In the end, he was able to help his mum buy her property and when she passed away, he inherited it.

I also met a couple from Lithuania who had bought a three-bedroom property. The wife told me that they lived with friends for a while whilst she and her husband saved up for a house. A few years later due to Brexit, they decided to move back to Lithuania. They sold their house for almost £400,000 and they had initially bought it for

£170,000. This was a strategic move which resulted in a big cash flow for them.

Environment as a whole

Our environment can at times be a catalyst for whether we become wealthy and live healthy lifestyles.

If you are surrounded by people who drink champagne every weekend, dress to impress and drive fancy cars to show off to friends, you may start to think that this is the norm. Then it becomes a habit which is too hard to shift and you then begin taking out loans because you want to fit in. As a result, you will continue to live a life of living, just to survive.

If this is your lifestyle, can you recognise it? A way to identify whether or not you are in this category is by asking yourself the following questions:

a. Are you having to borrow money to keep up with a certain lifestyle?
b. Do you have a plan for your money?

If you find yourself with no end goal for the money you are earning, then you are likely to continue living larger than what you can afford. You are therefore digging a hole for yourself rather than creating a solid foundation to keep yourself out of the rat race!

Money blocks - justifying your spending

An environment whereby everyone is practising living minimalist sounds great, but it can also be detrimental. Imagine walking into an environment where you feel guilty for having your nails done or buying a new outfit.

Usually, the first question a person asks you in an environment like that, if they see you in a new outfit is: *"How much did you pay for that?"* If the response to that question gets you feeling nervous and uncomfortable, you're likely to contemplate telling them the true price or lying about where it came from.

That type of environment has been created for you to think that you are not allowed to spend on luxury items and be proud of it, or that you need people's approval to spend on luxury goods. You should be bold, comfortable, and brave enough to be able to tell the truth.

I know that when I lived with my parents, I used to buy clothes at home, get my nails done and hair done. I would then come home very quietly, and literally tip toe up the stairs very slowly and hide the items so that my parents wouldn't see them or what I had done to my hair.

I knew that at first sight, the first questions they would ask would be *"Where did you get that? How much was it? You know you can get it cheaper?"* It would not be them telling me how great I looked, but over time, I had to get bold about my spending. Now my mother does her nails too because she also deserves to look and feel good.

Is this you? Do you feel uncomfortable or even guilty when you tell your family and friends how much you have spent when you come back from shopping? Have you been practising lies to say to them? Or are you the one who makes others feel bad about spending on luxury things?

This type of environment it can be harmful on one hand, it can help you spend less money, but it can also hinder your inner spirit to spend on what you love. It may even force you to become a liar as you may feel guilty for something you have not done. Remember that there is nothing wrong with treating yourself. To unblock this harmful way of thinking, is to have a spending plan that you are happy with and be bold enough to tell the truth. Walk in confidence because it is your prerogative to spend as you see fit, as long as it is within your means.

Negative talk

Environments whereby people talk negatively about wealthier people can also cause you to have negative thoughts about those that have more money than you. You then avoid becoming wealthy yourself. You unconsciously start creating money blocks which then stop you from receiving the riches you deserve.

A person who wants to grow in wealth would not destroy people. In fact, the more people you have on the planet, the more people you can serve or sell to. Also, the more products or services that get sold, the wealthier a person becomes.

If a person kills people decreases one's chances of having customers to serve. You should focus on how to build wealth and not become involved in gossip about how other people accumulated their wealth - it wastes your time and hinders your development and fortune.

In an article written by Dave Darby called *What's wrong with billionaires,*[25] it points out that some people may argue that billionaires damage the economy, destroy jobs, harm the community, damage nature and damage democracy. Whilst Device Rao stated in his article *Why do people hate billionaires* that:

> *'Many defenders point out that billionaires like Amazon's Jeff Bezos and the late Steve Jobs of Apple were able to make the daily lives of people easier through their world-changing businesses and technologies. Lehigh University professor Anthony O'Brien argues to The Morning Call that they, and others like them, make our lives better by introducing new products or by lowering the cost of existing products and that their success is not a result of their market power but of their spectacular success in satisfying consumer wants.'*[26]

Rachel Rodgers on her site *Hello Seven* also stated that:

> *'...Together, we can tip the balance of the world's economic and political power. ...No matter your*

25 Dave Darby, 2020. What's wrong with billionaires? [online] Available: *lowimpact.org/posts/whats-wrong-with-billionaires* [Accessed 28th Nov 2022].

26 Devika Rao, 2022. Why do people hate billionaires? [online] Available: *theweek.com/economy/1018418/why-do-people-hate-billionaires* [Accessed 28th Nov 2022]

*background, no matter what systemic injustices are stacked against you, you can make more money. You **deserve** to make more money and you know what? If this world is going to become a better place, you **NEED** to make more money.*'[27]

When you hear quotes like 'money is the root of all evil' and 'more money equals more problems' and fail to carry out your own research as to where these quotes come from, you could easily spend decades believing that wealthy individuals are evil and that the more money you have means the more problems you are going to get.

As a result, you can end up pursuing poverty rather than wealth and year after year, nothing changes because a lack of money gives you less options.

Trendy things

The deadly lie that some people have been taught is that being wealthy is about wearing the latest trendy clothes, trainers, gold chains and having flashy cars. This is absolutely not the case!

You will see most people being trendy on social media time and time again. When you watch television, the constant adverts, and the programmes that you watch can sometimes consist of the actors and actresses wearing the latest fashion items.

---

27 Rachel Rodgers, 2022: We should all be millionaires [online] Available: *helloseven.co/the-book*

Similarly, when you look at music videos, for example some rap videos, the lifestyle some might see is what some people will try to mimic. Kids as young as five years old start craving this lifestyle.

When you see a singer or a rap artist or any media personality wearing gold chains and driving fancy cars with catchy songs, you may not be able to stop your eyes from looking. The more you view these videos and images, the more you might continue to believe that this is what financial success looks like.

For example, in Salt-N-Pepa's video for their song *Push it*, do you see the gold chain around the girls' necks whilst they are dancing? This signifies wealth in some people's eyes, despite whether that was their intention or not.

There is absolutely nothing wrong with having fine gear as long as you have the means to buy it in the first place, or the means to get the money without robbing a bank, stealing it, or getting into debt for it. The question you should ask yourself is whether material wealth is the definition of true wealth? When I was a young teenager, I often heard that so and so was attacked by thugs for their Nike trainers. This is the reality which some of us lived in or are still living in.

This need of having to have the latest gear seeps into our minds, as well as our children. They then take it into schools and start demanding for these things such as the latest iPhone and the Nike trainers. Some of the things children demand off their parents cost more money than some people's rent in a month.

Friendships

Your friends can be the biggest influencers in your life and you may want to fit in or be unique amongst them. Some friends can be attracted to you because you look like cash due to what you are wearing and what you have. You can be blocked from making more money or even saving your money because of the type of friendships you have or lack of having the right friends with the right attitude about wealth creation.

I had very few close friends at a young age because I was never trendy. When my peers were wearing Nike shoes, I was wearing some not so-known shoes. In those days, being black and African was not cool at all and the headlines never helped. For instance, Children in Need always went back to Africa, in particular Uganda. This made me cringe when I saw the advert with a black child begging for food and the flies flying around them. It was not the image I wanted to see portrayed of my country.

My experience of Uganda was not that at all. whilst I lived with my grandparents, we lived in houses and watched TV after doing the chores. We always had food prepared from the garden and chicken, that we had to chase and prepare to cook on a stove.

In Tower Hamlets, my peers saw me and my siblings as poor African children, and my neighbours gave us clothes every now and again because that was their assumption. This was the stereotype they conformed to because of what they saw on TV.

It affected my relationships with other children in school and I was often alone. I became okay with not having friends constantly around me. I suppose you cannot miss what you never had in the first place.

I read more books and I began to formulate ideas like doing a school magazine and playing the saxophone during break times.

> 66 *Your friends can be the biggest influencers in your life and you may want to fit in or be unique amongst them.*

Did peer pressure affect me at times and how I viewed money? Of course, it did. I often found every excuse to not take part in physical education too, by creating excuses such as being on my period, because I did not have the latest trainers.

I had the physical build to do any sport and the teachers often picked me to represent the school in cross-country running and other sports activities. However, they could not understand why I would rather go to see my teacher in the business class, rather than participate in sports.

To combat peer pressure as a young person is hard, even harder if you are from a different country because you are learning not only about the world and its environment, but also about yourself. As you get older, it is very vital to know who you are, where you come from and where you are going. You must check in with yourself when you are slipping into self-doubt. Living in pretence is added pressure real wealthy people have no time for and neither should you.

Peer pressure can linger on even in adulthood, in your workplace and among your friends, hence why you may have a need to impress others that do not even matter. It is one thing to want to feel and look good but it's another when you pay for something you cannot afford.

Sometimes you may find yourself with fake friends. Those friends that say that they have money but do not have a penny to their name. You know the ones that are dressed in so much designer but cannot afford a taxi ride back home or the food at the restaurant. Those friends that invite you out but somehow leave it down to you to pay for the bill because they 'accidently' left their purse at home.

Networking is a great way to meet friends and create bountiful opportunities. It is essential to focus on networking with those people that will uplift your spirits, who are encouraging and can motivate you to be the best version of yourself.

Do not fear rejection from people, they may have never been the right people for you. It would help if you were among a cycle of friends and people who understand and are encouraging you to become successful in life, not those who make you feel unworthy. Your money will be blocked, not because you are not doing the right things but because you are among those that are not allowing you to grow internally and externally.

Peer pressure for status and respect

One of the biggest money blocks you may face in the community and perhaps globally is the need to have status, to have titles on your name. I am a public relations officer, I am a doctor, I am a nurse. Some people may even say that if you do not achieve those titles, you have failed.

You yourself may strive for these titles because they give you status and you would suddenly feel respected and accepted in society. As Lewis Howes would put it *'the titles give us prestige and credibility.'*[28]

When we first meet people at networking events, one of the first things they will ask is what you do for a living. We have no shame in telling them any title that suits us.

However, the need to be respected is so deep that you may fail to recognise that it is okay just to be you, give your name and a title that is in line with your purpose.

It is also an assumption that being a lawyer, doctor or minister means that one is wealthy. You'd be surprised that there are many lawyers that are not wealthy. Your need to fit in could be the money block, it could be the very thing that stops you from getting what you require to become fulfilled.

In How *I Make $27,000 / week with Passive income and productivity secrets*, Ali Abdaal, expressed his desire

---

28 Lewis Howes; 2021: How I Make $27,000/ Week with PASSIVE INCOME & Productivity Secrets | Ali Abdaal & Lewis Howes [online] Available: *youtube.com/watch?v=UJoZMuxx0T8&t=3271s* [Accessed 28 November 2022]

to be a teacher and a youtuber and how it excites him. He was also making much more money, than he did as a part-time doctor.

He was honest and transparent when he admitted, that although he made more money in what he loved doing, he felt that it was hard for him to give up his status as a doctor. He feared leaving his day job and held on to it as a form of security to make him feel good. He was asked whether being a doctor was his mission and he replied that being a teacher was.

It was concluded that Ali was holding on to the 'prestige and credibility' of being a doctor and this was costing him time and energy that he could redirect into what he enjoyed doing and was naturally good at.

Ali lived in fear of what people thought of him and we all do it to a certain extent. The question is: how deep is people pleasing embedded in you (if it is) and how much is it costing you in time and money? The interview showed us how conditioned our minds are into making us hold on to titles that clearly do not define who we really are.

What are you holding on to? Is it holding you back from pursuing your mission? In Ali's case he was fortunate enough to have found his gift and passion, which he turned into profit whilst he was still a part-time doctor.

What if you could do the same? What if you could let go of those titles and what people thought of you? The pressure to meet other people's expectations and your own views on how you should earn or even start earning money can cause you money blocks and slow down your process of gaining more money and living in your full potential.

During my years as an unemployed graduate, one of the things that I came across when I applied for roles was that I was either overqualified or the roles that I applied for weren't in my field. I would often be asked why I was applying for these jobs, when I could do something better.

This made me stop applying for those roles and it kept me unemployed even longer which led me into depression, anxiety, and less money in my pockets. I was too concerned about what people thought rather than the fact that I could do the jobs and I needed the money.

Another classic comment which your peers may make is when you finally get that role you have applied for, but your colleague then comes to you and says you should be using your degree to do something else. Or they may say this is not the place for you.

At law school, I had a lecturer who always reminded us that our degree was transferable in other fields and that we would not all become solicitors. This helped me to walk away from the legal field, however, trying to explain that to everyone else has always been challenging.

You cannot chase purpose without taking action. If you find yourself not knowing what your purpose is, then the best thing you can do, is to do any work that comes your way. You are likely to find your purpose whilst doing this.

For instance, if I never took on the opportunity to carry out group sessions on my day job. I would have never realised that I am a great coach, and that I could deliver programmes to thousands of people, transforming their lives for the better.

How history has created money blocks in certain cultures and how it determines how money is dealt with

On YouTube, I heard TD Jakes[29] on his teaching about being grounded in finance. He stated that due to slavery, black people in America worked for food and not for money and then they were freed and are now working for money but have no idea what to do with it.

This theory might be true and could justify why it has been said that the black community spend more than a trillion dollars on hair and makeup, compared to any other group of people. Surely, if this overspending on hair is not supporting this community in the long run, the black community owe it to themselves and their children to shift their mindset and learn how to manage finances so that they can live better lives for the next generations to come. The issue is that we live in a consumer - based society.

What about our white peers who have the same mentality? The ones who have decided that they are going to look like they have it all when they are actually living on credit card debt? The issue is never black and white or cultural. In fact, the issue is that you live in a consumer-

---

29 TD Jakes. 2016; Grounded in Finance [online] Available at: *dailymotion.com/video/x5c9ad8* [Accessed 28 November 2022]

based society which encourages you to want to buy, rather than be both a buyer and a seller.

It would help if you had an understanding that your mind may have been conditioned to think a certain way causing a wealth gap. You may have to work on reprogramming yourself, to build a better life for yourself and your community.

Empowering Women

Historically, men have been known to be the breadwinners and most societies have held the stereotypical view that women should stay at home and raise the children whilst men go out to work. This tradition made most men believe that they should be the only breadwinners.

It took World War One to highlight the fact that women can also go out to work and earn a living. It can be argued that in some cases, they do it even better than men. *'By mid-1943, almost 90% of single women and 80% of married women were working in factories or in the armed forces.'* Women no longer had to marry for money but were now able to marry for love.

This stereotypical view still holds strongly in most cultures, and it could be the reason why some women are not thriving and making more income than they are supposed to do. This leaves them to be enslaved by culture and traditions they had no say in creating in the first place.

Although more women now work, they are still cleaning, cooking, ironing, and helping their kids do their homework. By the time everything is done, it leaves them with no time to work on creating and building wealth in their spare times or to look after themselves.

It has been said repeatedly that men earn more than women and along with the stereotypical views some of us may hold in our subconscious mind, could it be that women are so grateful to get work that they fail to negotiate a better salary for themselves? Whilst men have historically been given the confidence to negotiate higher salaries because they have been taught that they can and that sky is the limit?

It is not about who to blame for the money blocks, however, it is about recognising that the money blocks hinder your progress. You must take action by empowering yourself to be financially literate in every area and recognising that some traditions, culture, and beliefs may not serve you the way you are supposed to be served. It's not a question of changing other people's minds. It's rather acknowledging that you may have to drop some practises that are clearly impractical and try new approaches for a chance to succeed in the area of finance.

I want to think that I am an open minded individual. If I hear that you're practising something that is helping you create wealth and live a healthy lifestyle, I am willing to learn and evaluate the pros and cons and impact it will have on my life and then try to implement it. After all, I deserve to prosper and so do you.

Does your environment equip you to earn more and be more right now? Do you need to evaluate your environment and culture and historical background with how you deal with money in more details, rather than allow or take on anything that has been directly or indirectly passed down to you from generation to generation? Is it time you got rid of those negative cultural thoughts that are not benefiting you?

Are you ready to break the generational curse that has stopped you and your families from achieving a high level of financial success and fulfilment?

Debt - There is always a way out

Debt is a clear money block for most people. For others, it's used as a stepping stone to increase one's income by using the debt to buy assets or produce products and services to create other sources of income.

"The average UK adult is £30,575 in debt – and that's without student loans."[30]

I believe that with the correct information and tools, you can get out of debt quicker and faster so that you focus on fulfilling your full potential.

Debt, loans or money borrowed - this is when one borrows money on the promise of giving it back soon or on a specific date. It gets more complicated because some debts have interest rates attached to them, which means that you will end up paying more than the original amount.

A debt can be secured on an asset that you may own or unsecured, which can be in the form of credit cards, car loans,

---

30 Bank of England, 2021. What do I need to know about debt [online] Available at: *bankofengland.co.uk/knowledgebank/what-do-i-need-to-know-about-debt* (Accessed 26th January 2023)

personal loans, store cards, etc. Failing to pay bills such as gas, electric, council tax and rent can stack up your debt.

The Bank of England stated that: '*Most people would struggle to pay upfront for things that help them improve their lives such as a house, a car or a degree. So debt isn't necessarily bad but as we've seen in the past, such as when the financial crisis happened, it can be.*'[31]

Not being able to pay upfront means that your income or savings are not enough to purchase those things that you want and you hope can improve your life.

Not being able to pay back loans or even failing to pay for bills can affect our credit score and has a major impact on our ability to purchase big items such as buying a home or even renting. It can also affect taking out contracts for mobile phones and taking out loans to start a business.

If you take out a loan and you are able to keep up with the repayments then it's great because, it will help to improve your credit score and improve your relationship with the lenders. They are more likely to borrow you even more money.

Why do we take out debt?

The reason could be that 'we sometimes swim with sharks because we are trying to get to our destiny quicker than the next person.'

---

31 Bank of England, 2021. What do I need to know about debt [online] Available at: *bankofengland.co.uk/knowledgebank/what-do-i-need-to-know-about-debt* (Accessed 26th January 2023)

You may take out debt for various reasons. One could be because you see an opportunity that will help improve your life it could be because you are desperate for change, therefore you decide to seek for a bank loan to help make this opportunity come true.

You ask for the loan because you also believe in your mind or by your calculation, that you will be able to pay the money back.

Debt can be a good debt when everything falls into place, but it can be detrimental to you when life happens and believe me it does.

Life events such as a death in a family, a divorce, a newborn or just a mere tragedy can spark feelings inside of you that may lend you to taking out even more debt or stop you from earning the money you need to pay off the debt.

Debt can be considered to be bad because it's a promise to pay back the loan based on someone's past experience and not on future events that might occur. It is a risk you take based on an assumption that everything will be as it is now.

When you take out a loan in the hope of paying it back, your brain tells the lender and yourself that provided that your life stays the same for the next few years, you will be able to pay this debt back. It's a risk because you cannot predict the future. Guess what? The bank knows this hence why you are charged interest on the loan you may decide to take out.

The high interest on the loan is an indication of the fact that the lender believes that you're a big risk and the chances of you not being able to pay them back the loan is high, rather than low.

For instance, due to being bullied at work and the mere thought of getting up in the morning to go to work in the toxic environment killing me inside, I took out a £30,000 loan which worked out to be £50,000 after 12.1% interest was added.

I had indirectly taken away my choice of being able to walk away from the toxic environment because I took on extra responsibilities that relied on me keeping that job for longer.

Now I had no choice but to suck it up, get up to go to work and face the people that belittled me. They made me feel unworthy by telling me that my work was not good enough, even after I had won an award for my achievements.

In those moments, you forget why you even took out the loan in the first place. Whilst other people would say things like if you're not happy in the company or they are not treating you right, walk away, the truth is you can't because too many variables are relying on you to bring in that income. This right here is the rat race which can lead to you breaking down into pieces. This can also open up a floodgate of tears.

Humans cannot foresee the future - you can only prepare for it.

Good debt vs. Bad debt

You may label debt as being either good or bad. Good debt is described as a debt you have taken out to purchase an asset which would eventually go up in value, so that you are able to pay off the debt and make a profit from it. This is called leveraging your debt. An example of this is when you buy a house or start a viable business.

Even good debt can turn into bad debt. If that asset depreciates in value, then you might end up making a loss or fail to generate a profit. Taking out a debt or loan is a financial risk which can cripple you for a lifetime - the risk must be calculated and even then, nothing is guaranteed.

It can be debatable as to whether property is the best asset to have because the value of properties have always at most times gone up in value. The question remains that if property is a such a great asset, then why did millions of people lose their homes during both the 2008 recession and the 2020 pandemic?

My conclusion is that those who were unfortunate enough to lose their homes, were probably living pay cheque to pay cheque and were not able to survive for even more than a month after the loss of their income. When a crisis hits us like the recession or pandemic, it becomes almost impossible to hold on to material wealth, whilst trying to meet your basic needs.

We pretty much underestimate our circumstances and the events that can derail us. As a result of this, some people end up living on the edge by taking out debts and fail to save for emergencies.

The best way to deal with a money block such as debt is to ask yourself: where are you at present with this debt?

1. Are you considering taking out a loan?
2. Have you got a loan and if so, are you paying the minimum?
3. Have you got debts and letters demanding for repayments which you are unable to pay for because your circumstances have changed?
4. Have you already been given court letters and county court judgments?
5. Are you now debt free?

If you are debt free, then congratulations, because it feels so good to be free! You may want to read this chapter so that you can have an awareness of the things you can do to avoid debt or to pay it off quickly (if you find yourself in these circumstances).

It's important to understand why you accumulate debt in the first place before you begin the journey of becoming debt free. You should examine your thoughts and understand your behaviour patterns.

I got into debt because I took out student loans and I spent money on law books so that I could do my best to pass my law degree. As a result, I received a 2:1 and then I topped it up with the professional studies loan. One of the mistakes I made was listening to my cousin, who advised me to leave my part-time job to focus on law school.

There was nothing wrong with the advice I was given, but I did not take my situation into consideration. The problem was that I failed to look at the fact that I had to repay back the money I owed, so leaving my part-time job was not a smart option.

I also naively believed that with my qualifications, I could easily get a well-paid job and pay back the loans.

If you are in debt and you are aware that life happens, you should take action to pay off the debt quickly. This will save you interest and gives you both power and control over your money.

If you find yourself in a position whereby you feel that you need to take that risk and take out that loan, then you have to try and assess your appetite for that risk. This means doing the maths and adding up the interest charged on the loan.

If you're stuck in debt, there are a number of things you can do according to your situation and your needs.

66 *You should examine your thoughts and understand your behaviour patterns*

Free support

In the U.K, if you are unemployed and have no assets or savings over £16,000, you can contact the National Debt Line, Citizen's Advice Bureau (CAB) and Christians

Against Poverty. There are also other free debt management companies that are recognised by the financial services – check them out at *moneysavingexpert.com*.[32]

When I volunteered at the Citizen Advice Bureau, I worked as a generalist advisor and advised individuals who were in debt. The CAB had a debt package and sample letters that one could use to contact their creditors.

Be aware that debts are divided into either priority debt or non-priority debt. For example, council tax would come in the priority group and bank loans would come into the non-priority group. Therefore, it is good to distinguish your debts between the priority debts and non-priority debts.

Before contacting the creditors, it is important to draw up a budget that shows your expenses daily, monthly, and yearly.

This is when having a budget of some form is useful because creditors look at that budget to assess your capability in being able to pay off the loan. You can do this by using your past bank statements - they will show you what your essential bills are and your non-essential expenses.

You can get examples of budgets in the Citizen Advice Bureau debt packs; you might be able to find a budget sheet on the Money Savings Expert website or even Google.

At this point, a basic budget would show your income minus your expenditure and the amount left over. After prioritising your debts, you can start distributing the amount

---

32 Founder, Martin Lewis. Editor -Chief, Marcus Herbert 2022 Cutting your costs, fighting your corner. [online] Available at: *moneysavingexpert.com*

you have left to the creditors, making a proposal based on your budget. If you can only afford £1 a month then propose it to the leader. It's a great start.

The courts look at whether or not you have attempted to pay something and are planning to pay the money back before they take further action.

If you have an asset and have savings above £16,000, most free services will not support you.

Debt free methods

You should think of ways to reduce your debts quickly so that you can focus on prosperity especially if you have income coming in.

I will discuss three methods that I have used to help myself, however, these methods are just recommendations. You have to decide what method to use and what works well according to your personality and capability. It is also wise to get an accountability partner because this journey can be trying.

It is important to prioritise your debts according to the impact they will have on you. An example of how you can prioritise your debt is that of a credit card loan v your student loan. The credit card loan may take precedence over a student loan since a student loan has no bearing on your credit history and does not stop you from getting a mortgage or getting a mobile phone contract. Above all debts, the council tax may be the priority debt that must be paid off first because the council (in my experience), don't negotiate before taking you to court.

Your credit card debt does impact on your credit score and can prohibit you from taking up other loans to support your projects that could lead to new opportunities.

Method 1 - Debt settlement [33]

You could try a debt settlement plan. This requires you to have a lump sum of money that you can pay the creditors. This will reduce the amount you pay back towards the debt.

The lump sum can come from an inheritance, gift or a sale of items. You can contact the lenders yourself and let them know that you would like to make a payment.

Debt settlement method cuts down on the debt and any interest incurred and it's faster and quicker. The lenders have to agree to it and you also have to have the lump sum of money.

The main focus here is getting the lump sum. When I used the debt settlement method, it worked for the overdraft debts I had once I was able to save up a lump sum. I then called up the creditors and asked for the debt to be settled.

For example, if you have a debt of £21,000, you could ask the lender how much it would be for you to pay off the lump sum today. They may respond by saying that you would

---

33 Step Change Debt charity, 2022, Putting together a full and final settlement offer [online] Available at: *stepchange.org/debt-info/settlement-offers-to-creditors.aspx* [Accessed 29th November 2022]

need to pay £15,000. If you have the £15,000, you would have saved yourself £5,000 and you'd also be debt-free.

Method 2 - The avalanche method

Another way of getting rid of debt is by using the avalanche method.[34]

1. It requires you to have extra money coming in, you could find the extra money by cutting down on expenses or getting another income stream from a side hustle or a part time job.
2. You must list the debts in order of the one that has the highest interest rates first.
3. You then put the extra money towards the debt with the highest interest rate loan and continue to pay the minimum amount on all the other debts.
4. Once the debt has been paid off, you then take the minimum amount you were paying on that debt as well as the extra and add it on the next debt with the highest interest until all the debts are paid off.

The point of this method is to pay off the debt faster and pay less interest. However, many have argued that it requires discipline, and it also assumes that you will always be able to get the extra amount of money, which may not be possible for you depending on your circumstances.

---

34 Wells Fargo,2022. Comparing the snowball and the avalanche methods of paying down debt [online] Available at: _wellsfargo.com/goals-credit/smarter-credit/manage-your-debt/snowball-vs-avalanche-paydown/#:~:text=In%20contrast%2C%20the%20%22avalanche%2_ [Accessed 29t[h] November 2022]

Method 3 - The snowball method

The third method you could consider is called the snowball method.[35]

1. You would need to first save up for an emergency fund. Dave Ramsey would recommend $1000 in the UK (at the time of writing this was equivalent to £715.81).
2. You then list your debts in the order of smallest to largest.
3. You then have to find extra cash by either cutting down on your bills and costs or getting a side hustle along with the job that you're doing.
4. Whilst continuing to pay the minimum on all the debts, you then take the smallest debt first and add the extra income on top, using it to pay off the smallest debt.
5. You then move on to the next debt and add the amount that you were paying on the first debt, including the extra amount and continue the process until all the debts are gone.

Starting with the small debt allows you to see what you want, what you may have thought was impossible suddenly becomes possible. The small wins encourage you to continue the process.

---

35 D. Ramsey, 2003 The Total Money Makeover Work Book, Nashville, Tennessee: Thomas Nelson

The quicker you pay off your debt, the better. In the long run, you will pay less interest and you will get out of debt before life gets in the way.

When I first used the snowball method, I didn't know how it would work in the U.K.

I read my loan agreements and I saw that they had added in the agreement that if you wanted to, you could pay extra on your debt. It required me having to call the creditors. I had to be specific with the amount I wanted to add and where I wanted it to go.

I wanted £500 to be added to the principal amount, which in return reduced the actual loan and not the interest left to be paid each month. I reduced my £50,000 loan down to £17,000 within less than two years. It felt great.

I accumulated the extra income by renting out my property and getting an agreement from the lender.

I couldn't settle the loan as quickly as I wanted to but it gave me a boost. I can say that the method worked.

To use the snowball method, you must find the extra cash to pay towards the smallest debt and before you pay it off, you must call the creditors and instruct them to put the extra amount towards the principal debt.

Debt settlement is probably the quickest and cheapest, in terms of how much interest you will pay. The avalanche method also allows you to pay off your debt soon and with less interest than the snowball method.

However, out of the three methods, the snowball method is easy to do because it allows you to have small wins quicker and faster. This should encourage you to continue with the process. It is hard enough to start paying off the debt with more than the minimum but to sustain the journey until the end, takes willpower and determination. This is what the snowball method can give you.

The one thing that these methods fail to account for is that life has its ups and downs and when an emergency happens, you may need to redirect the amount you are spending on the debt, towards the actual crisis.

Dave Ramsey (an advocate for the snowball method), believes that before using the method, you must save the lump sum of $1000 for emergencies. This is a great idea but some emergencies cost more, and you must be aware of this and prepare for those emergencies.

My tip is that after you have decided what method to use from the above three:

Consider growing the emergency account over a £1000 threshold whilst paying for the debt.

This does two things:

- It covers the immediate emergency.
- It covers unexpected bills that might cause you to take another loan to pay off the actual bill.

You must also put aside some 'fun' money just in case there are opportunities you may want to take up. This could give you a balance and you may feel less emotional and less deprived about the process.

It is challenging to be disciplined for a year or more, so I urge you to get an accountability partner - a person who wants to see you win and understands your needs and pain.

Paying off your mortgage debt quickly

After reading David Bach's book *The Automatic Millionaire*,[36] I came across this concept of a biweekly mortgage. This is when you agree with the lender that you would like to pay for your mortgage every two weeks instead of every month.

For example, instead of paying £600 a month for a mortgage, you pay £300 every fortnight. This cuts down on the interest rate faster because interest rate is added on daily not monthly.

If the lender is unable to do it, you can pay 10% more on your monthly mortgage and you will get results either way. You must let the banks know that you wish to pay the extra amount towards the principal amount off the mortgage.

Paying off your mortgage earlier than agreed can at times incur charges, so it is wise to check your loan agreement or mortgage agreement, to see how much you are able to pay off in advance without being charged.

My journey into debt

The first loan I ever took out was a student loan and the banks offered me an overdraft, a credit card and a free phone.

---

36 D Bach, 2004. *The Automatic millionaire — A Powerful one step plan to live and finish rich*. London: Penguin Group

I thought that after law school I would get a job to pay it all off. It never occurred to me that getting a high-paying job was going to be even more challenging than getting a degree or completing law school.

I learnt how to study; however, I had no strategy on how I should get into the job market and not only pay back the money I owed, but also fulfil my full potential and prosper at the same time. I was financially illiterate. As a student, I could see that I created a bubble with no real plan of how to manifest that faith and become the person that I intended to be.

Fear

After purchasing my first home, I borrowed money to make sure that the house was hospitable. It was a 1900s home and it did not have radiators or a toilet inside.

I wanted to save up money to renovate the house, which would have taken months if not years. On one cold January day, one of the hardest working, dedicated members of staff were fired for protecting the company from a fraudulent activity. Out of fear that I might get fired just like he did, I quickly took out the first loan offer I got, without looking at the interest rate and the impact it would have on my finances.

In fact, the fear also stemmed from the fact that this was not the first time I had witnessed a dedicated member of staff being fired, it was the second time. Although the gentleman in the first instance had a nice pay out for being wrongly dismissed, it affected me mentally.

At that moment, I thought that this could happen to me at any time and the last thing I wanted was to have an incomplete house. I felt that I had to move fast. Although a colleague told me not to take out the loan, I did not listen. My fear was real in my head and having been put on PIP more than once, I could not see it any other way.

I called the estate agent that helped me to buy the house for help. He told me that this was the only offer I could get, and I ended up with a £50,000 loan (which I thought would be £30,000). I failed to pay attention to the small details which was the amount of interest that was added on to the loan. Although the company had advertised 6% interest; this was only for the chosen few and I was certainly not one of them. In fact, my interest on the loan was doubled.

I had dealt myself the wrong cards. I was saved by the fact that I had a plan on how I was going to pay off the loan, which was to rent the property out with the bank's permission to pay for the cost of the loan. This meant living with my parents for an extended period.

Throughout my journey, I knew one thing that I had learnt that I wanted the world to know. Having money gives you the confidence to be able to defend yourself. I began to read books about finances, and I also attended the Stewardship course. This is when I discovered the snowball method which helped reduce that loan quickly.

Fear, worry and anxiety are some of the reasons why you might make crippling decisions, such as taking out debts that you may not be able to pay back. I was fortunate that my mother was happy for me to stay in her house with my children but I know that many people do not have that resource. I wanted to buy a home for myself to live in, not to rent out. I suppose that this was never God's plan - it was my plan, and His plans always prevail.

In fact, renting the property has allowed me to help my family and take care of my father when he really needed me. It also helped me discover my purpose and be able to deliver on that purpose. I was able to see through the mess I had created out of fear and turn a situation that could have been negative into a positive one.

Are you in debt? If so, how did you get into debt? Can you recall the first time you took out a loan and what was your reason? What is your current plan to get out of debt and step into your greatness?

As a human being you have the power to reassess your situation and dig yourself out of it. Try to see the positives in your situation and find ideas on how you can climb out of the rabbit hole that you may have found yourself in. Please don't give up; keep on ploughing away because a solution is near.

You can do something about your situation, but this means being open and willing to make sacrifices for the things you want. Staying in my parents' home was a sacrifice I made, to create a little heaven for myself and a legacy for my children.

How do you overcome the money block that halts your ability to create more abundance in your life?

We all want to create more wealth in our lives and live our best life to the fullest. To do so, you may have to create a pool of wealth by either selling something or providing a service. Your money block could be that you might be too scared of charging the actual price you want to charge for your products and services. That fear can stop you from earning the money you deserve.

You might fear coming across as being greedy. It is mind-boggling how you can be so fearful of charging customers the actual price for your products or services yet be willing to pay full fees for other people's services and products.

Why you could be afraid of wanting more for yourself

I recall Patrice Washington, stating in one of her programmes *Purpose to Platform*:

'*Do you ever hear the gas station announcing or warning us before they increase their prices? Yet we accept the increase. We go out and buy petrol because we need it. Then why are we so frightened of charging what we are really worth?*'

You are simply devaluing yourself every time you undercharge for your products and services or, are too afraid to ask clients to pay more money for those services.

You may catch yourself saying things like 'I can do it on my own,' or 'the Lord will provide.' Because you have been conditioned to not ask for money but be a consumer. You then become so comfortable in your own lies and become unwilling to change, so you then make up every excuse to keep you in your bubble.

You are not going to get any more money unless you ask for it and if you fail to ask then you should not get mad, envy or be jealous of John who is now a millionaire and charges £4,000 for his products, whilst you are still at £350 per client. John knows his worth. Do you know your true value in society?

You also need to ask yourself a question: why are you undercharging? How are you ever going to serve people when your bank accounts are empty?

Did you know that if items or products are too cheap, buyers have it in their minds that it must be of low quality? Waitrose charge full prices on items and Apple charge over £1000 for their products because they know they are worth it. You do not dispute the price tag even if it costs more than your rent for the month because their products are awesome. So are you.

You have to learn to appreciate money by not being afraid to value your goods and services appropriately.

You are not being greedy when you ask for more - greedy people are people who act unethically immoral. If you know that you are serving from the heart and to the best of your abilities, then why can't you value your services accordingly?

If you undervalue your time and service, you are surely being dishonest and make no mistake of it. You will lose out on making the kind of money you need to support those who really need your help in society. Without money your voice can easily be silenced, however, if you become a billionaire your voice would be heard clearly. This way, you are more likely to make a more significant impact on the world.

10 Key Points – Empower in overcoming money blocks

1. You must know your worth; this means that you must stop devaluing yourself.
2. Prioritise your expenses so that you can focus on fulfilling your full potential.
3. Take only the risk that you can manage when things go wrong and analyse your return on investment.
4. Evaluate who you are and what you value the most in your environment.
5. Become financially literate - this means reading and taking classes.
6. Don't be afraid to want to change or want more for yourself and the generations to come.
7. Practice best practices (stop following norms for the sake of preserving culture if it's not supporting your overall wellbeing).

8. Continue always to check on yourself to make sure that you're not slipping back into habits that are not supporting your growth.
9. Your money is God's money; He needs you to manage it well.
10. Remember that you have the resources to fulfil your full potential in life.

> 66 *Your money is God's money;*
> *He needs you to manage it well.*

CHAPTER 4

Empower in Savings

"Strive to live, not just to survive"
— **Sandra Kaima**

I recall hearing someone saying that you must ask yourself one of the most important questions today: if you lost your earnings, how long would you be able to sustain your lifestyle before your money runs out?

In the UK, you have the welfare system that gives you a limited amount of support until you find work. However, if you have been earning X amount of money and are used to having excellent quality goods and luxuries, like going on multiple holidays without worrying about money coming in the following month, you would struggle to become accustomed to a system that pays you a minimum amount of money.

If you can have more, why would you settle for less?

Saving is therefore crucial to our success in striving to live, having freedom of choice and fulfilling our full potential, rather than just surviving pay cheque to pay cheque.

Why do you want to save?

Saving your money gives you options and as the saying goes 'cash is king.' If you want to feel empowered, have a renewed sense of confidence and live in abundance, you have to be able to enjoy your money and learn also to keep it so that it works for you.

Equipment and appliance

Imagine waking up in the morning and reaching out for your phone. You're trying to scroll through all your messages, but your phone is not responding and has stopped working. You try charging it but there is no power. You even go to the mobile shop to speak to the man who repairs phones, but he says it's unfixable and that you will have to buy a new phone. According to your calculations, you only have £350 spare cash in the account and you have no other money coming in until the end of the month. That money is already accounted for because you have to go to a wedding soon and you need a new outfit.

The guy in the shop tells you that the cheapest, good-quality, second hand phone is £450 and you can't get a phone contract phone because you don't have good credit.

Can you relate?

It's still Sunday morning and you decide to pop downstairs to open the fridge-freezer and the milk is off. Why? The fridge isn't working and that's another £300-400 to dish out.

Then you try using the washing machine and it starts flashing an error code which you look up on Google. It says that this error code means your washing machine is beyond repair and you need a new one.

You see, on top of paying for everyday costs such as rent and regular bills, you have daily appliances and equipment you use to simplify your life.

If you have the extra cash to buy the new equipment and appliances you require at home, then great, because most people don't. The problem can spiral even further if you decide to take out loans from loan sharks, get into bank overdrafts or borrow money from family and friends to pay for equipment which is not guaranteed to last.

What makes it worse is the thought of calling your friend to moan about how awful your Sunday is going. It stays a thought because the whole situation is making you feel too embarrassed. You don't have money to repair or restore your things and you then remember that your phone doesn't work, so you couldn't call your friend to vent, even if you wanted to.

You decide to double check your savings account, but you find that the account has less than £100 pounds because you forgot to pay into it consistently.

The money you have is just enough to pay for the petrol to go to work. Now you wish you had insured those items because you could surely do with some help.

You are now dreading going to work on Monday morning because not only do you not have enough money until payday, but the kids have also only eaten half the toast and the rest has been tossed in the bin.

You react by yelling at them to not waste the food and that money doesn't grow on trees. Your stress levels are high and you are blaming the whole world for how unfair the system is. You refuse to look in the mirror and change your ways. You then look at your hands and remember that you spent £25 on a new set of nails. You then retouched your hair and added on the natural weaves which costed £850.

Your smooth shiny legs also now remind you of the fact that you spent £60 waxing your whole-body last Saturday and of course the kids' hairdos costed an extra £25 each. You then spent £150 on brand new shoes and gear for the kids so that they feel and look comfortable. £250 on food and drink ready for the week ahead... the list is endless.

You are now frustrated, anxious and concerned with yourself and wonder how unfair this is. How on earth could you have allowed this situation to happen? You look good but feel lousy and ugly all at the same time.

Saving your money is important because you can have spare cash to pay for your basic needs in the home and other new opportunities. The truth is you have no idea as to when the fridge is going to break down; or the cooker or washing machine.

Neither can you predict the future. However, you can try and prepare for it by creating a system that considers eventualities. There's nothing wrong with spending on what you love but it's great to be able to look ahead to protect what you love and what loves you the most by saving some of your money.

Just the other day, a close friend of mine sent me a text, whilst at a garage and said that the repairs on his car are going to cost him £600. He then texts an hour later and said that they have found another problem which is going to cost him an additional £500. Whilst I was dying with laughter, he urged for me to call him an ambulance (in jest). It immediately reminded me of why it was pivotal to save money. Unexpected expenses can hurt your pockets and leave you boiling inside with rage. He managed to pay for the repairs, only to have a car crash weeks after. As a result, the car was damaged beyond repair but gladly, he was alive.

You have most probably heard that you must set up an emergency fund which can be used to meet your immediate needs. So, I suggest that you consider putting away cash for a long-term emergency fund to protect you from unforeseen situations or just in case you lose your home.

The Covid-19 pandemic and recession have shown that your earnings can stop at any time, therefore it's great to strive for multiple income streams and also put some cash aside to ride out those unexpected bumps in your path.

Why save?

Saving money allows you to be able to buy assets that would in return yield ongoing income. In the book *Rich*

Dad, Poor Dad,[37] it permeated in my head that it is so important to have an asset that creates a passive income to help with your cost-of-living expenses. However, to build the assets, you need to save, or find the capital. Or be in a great position to borrow money from banks and create that asset, but no bank is going to lend you money if you are living on the edge.

Do you want to start a business?

Imagine waking up on a Monday morning, with a vision to start your own business. Your business cannot be realised if you have no cash even to buy the basics. If you want to start up your own business today or someday, then start to save for it now. The more you can save, the better. It gives you independence from lenders such as the banks and it gives you a head start for that business. Getting a loan is not a bad thing, but the risk has to be calculated and having your own savings puts you in the driving seat of your business.

Do you want to move out of your parents' home?

You have decided that it is time for you to move out and this is a big move. Before you start looking for where you are going to live, you should first ask yourself, how much money do you need to have? How long will it last before

---

37 Kiyosaki, R T. 2017. Rich Dad Poor Dad, 3rd Edition – 20th Anniversary edition, United Stated of America: Plata Publisher. LLC

you run out of it? If you are going to rent, then that's okay, but have you have saved up a deposit along with a few months of rent to pay the landlord?

My guidance to anyone who wants to move out is to do the following:

1. To find work.
2. To try and create several passive income streams.
3. To **save, save, save before** moving out.

The money saved would in return help you buy a home, because purchasing a home can be cheaper than renting in the long run. It is also an asset for life; this makes your financial foundation much more solid giving you options.

For example, if a young person at the age of 20, earned even as little as £1300 a month and decided to spend £250 on themselves, a further £250 to contribute to household bills, they would be left with £800. They could save for 12 months - multiply that to 5 years. £9600 x 5 years = £48,000 which could go towards a deposit for a house or a business. If you turn that into 10 years, you will have a whooping £96,000 by the age of 30. This money can be used for investing so that you can start earning more money on top of more money, creating passive income leading to financial empowerment.

Saving to have options in life

Saving money empowers us, renews our confidence, and creates a life of abundance. In return, you get options to buy and receive the things you need in life. Such as being able to have options to whether you get private treatment at the dentist or hospital or stay on the NHS waiting list for two years to get treatment. An option to whether you live in a rough neighbourhood or a beautiful neighbourhood and you get to decide whether your child stays in a public school or goes to private school.

A friend of mine was diagnosed with cancer, she told me that she had to wait six months for treatment on the NHS. However, because she owned her house, she was able to take £50,000 equity from her home to receive the cancer treatment much quicker than waiting on the NHS for treatment. Because she had that asset she had the option to receive treatment quicker rather than wait six months.

Saving for retirement

Whilst listening to BBC radio 4 a few years ago, I recall hearing an interview between two elderly ladies. One was on state benefit and the other one had a private pension. The two elderly ladies showed us the difference between a person who has worked and saved for a private pension and another one relying on state pension. The person who had paid into a private pension received more money and went on multiple holidays during retirement, while the person who relied on a state pension alone could not afford to do that with the money they had. She had to be frugal with every penny she received from the state.

In the *Automatic Millionaire* book,[38] David Bach, says you have to '*pay yourself first and then make it automatic.*'[39] This means that you have to invest in yourself first before you start paying off for other things. This means putting the maximum amount of money away into your private or employers pension scheme. This is a sure way to get monetary rich.

Why you may find it difficult to save – the lies you could be telling yourself

Lie number one - that you are not earning enough

You may find it hard to save because you may think that you are not earning enough.

Therefore, you strive to earn more and as a result you burn out because you are now working over 40 hours a week to earn that extra money. However, you end up spending even more money on take away foods because you have no time to cook, and on maintenance to repair your overworked body.

It's been stated in so many books and shown that the more you earn, the more you spend and as a consequence of that, you start to believe that you are not earning enough.

---

38 D Bach, 2004. *The Automatic millionaire — A Powerful one step plan to live and finish rich*. London: Penguin Group

39 D Bach, 2004. *The Automatic millionaire — A Powerful one step plan to live and finish rich*. London: Penguin Group p 82

I know a friend of mine who works as an administrator. She earns £1500 a month and saves £500 by living a frugal life. She put her extra income towards a deposit for a house.

She let the money grow for several years and she eventually had enough money to apply for a mortgage. She is now on her second property.

In the meantime, her close friend earned over £6,000 a month and used her money to go on extravagant holidays. In her response, she said that she needed the breaks to release the pressure from her work. She also bought costly cosmetics which promised to keep her skin soft and radiate and said that she found it difficult to save any money. She was not able to save a deposit for a property, although she desperately wanted to.

You see, you may often assume that it is hard to save because you are not earning enough. The truth is it is probably more than enough, but you choose to spend the money irresponsibly. You may fail to prioritise and set boundaries to what is really important to you.

The more we earn, the more we need because we associate money with numbers, not on how we feel. Melissa Leong wrote in the Financial Post that Michael Norton who teaches at Harvard Business School and authored *Happy Money: The Science of Smarter Spending*, was able to recently survey high network Britons (individuals who had a net worth of more than $1 million). He asked them how happy they were on a scale of one to 10 and how much money they would need to be a perfect 10. Everybody said two to three times as much money. He concluded that there was a problem because people who had $1 million said 'If I had $3 million, I'd be a perfect 10.' Then the people who had $3 million said, 'If I had $9-million, I'd be a perfect 10.'[40]

People thought that increasing their income would make them happier, even those on an average income thought the same, but in fact it would not. It was found that having experiences was what made people happy; of course, experiences cannot be counted like money can.

I believe that even if you won the lottery, you would struggle to save your money, unless you learnt how to save. Most lottery winners end up with no money within a few years. They end up broke, not because they never had enough money, but because they lacked financial literacy and did not have a system in place that supported their earnings.

Having a lot of money does not change your bad habits, all it does is exuberate your behaviour with money, whether good or bad. Therefore, the first thing that you should do is create a system, no matter how much you earn and stick with it.

In his book *Atomic Habits*, James Clear states: '*If you want better results, then forget about setting goals. Focus on your system instead.*'[41]

---

40 Melissa Leong, 2014. Why do we spend what Science says about our personal finances [online] Available at: *financialpost.com/personal-finance/ why-do-we-spend-what-science-says-about-our-personal-finances* [Accessed 2021]

41 C, James, 2018. *Atomic Habits—An Easy and Proven Way to Build Good Habits and Break Bad Ones: Tiny Changes, Remarkable Results.* Penguin Random House, London p 28

Lie number two – we were never taught how to save money

Parents and your environment also play a part on how you deal with your money, but as you get older, you have to make your own decisions and choose whether to teach yourself the lessons you never learnt. Some ways to do this are by reading books, getting coaching and putting into practice what you have learnt. This may mean making sacrifices and hard decisions about your life and what you are going to change or stick with, rather than blaming your parents who only passed on what they knew at the time and the limited knowledge they were exposed to.

One Sunday morning, whilst I was attending a Catholic Church, one of the priests told us a story about two brothers who were born with an alcoholic father. He stated that one decided to drink like his father as this was all he knew, but the other child was reluctant to continue his father's bad habits and swore never to drink. Ultimately, it's you who has to define your success, your route and what bad habits you're willing to hold on to.

The truth: you may have never been taught how to think ahead

It is pivotal to learn how to think ahead. The first time I came across the term was when I was learning how to drive, and the driving instructor said to me that I had not been taught to think ahead. What he meant was that my mind had not been programmed to watch out for hazards and incidents. This is precisely what the hazard and perception test prepares us for before we take our practical test on the road.

You must teach yourself to think ahead and apply the same thought process to your finances and other areas of your life. Saving your money requires you to think about those circumstances that may incur which you cannot foresee or which you can foresee but don't have a time frame for. It empowers you to manage the downturns, the downfalls and any hiccups along the way. You are therefore able to avoid the pitfalls allowing you to have control over your finances.

Thinking ahead also prepares you for the emotional times such as having a death in the family, the frustrations, anxiety and sudden mood swings. When you think ahead, you can handle the pain better than if you were not prepared. It allows you to take up new opportunities and you protect yourself and the next generation to come. Saving for the future means that you are taking responsibility rather than allowing someone else to control your destiny. The future can be unpredictable; therefore, it is wise to prepare for it.

Lie number three - all you need to do is have faith

Praying will prepare you for the battle but faith without works will not be enough. Saving aggressively and intentionally takes work and sometimes having to make sacrifices. Real freedom comes from within. If you want success in your finances then pray for mercy, gratitude, peace, and perseverance because you will need grace and faith to maintain a good balance.

Lie number four - things are too expensive

Prices are forever on the rise and some will argue that they are rising much higher and faster than wages. It would help if you asked yourself a few questions such as:

1. Who is successful and prospering in these challenging times?
2. What are they doing that is different from what you are doing?
3. How are they dealing with the rise of inflation and what sacrifices are they making?
4. What sacrifices are you willing to make?
5. What will you spend less on and save?
6. Do you have to downsize and live-in a less expensive flat or house?
7. Do you have to move back home with your parents and cut down on costs?

You may find it difficult to save, because saving money means making changes that you may not be willing to make. True story, a friend of mine, wanted quick advice on how to continue paying for his mortgage. When I suggested that he should consider renting one of the rooms in the house, he blew my head off and was disgusted by the thought. He was adamant that he could not live with a stranger. The other option was for him to find extra money quickly or to stay building up mortgage arrears, which would eventually lead up to his home being repossessed by the mortgage lenders.

66 *The truth: you may have never been taught how to think ahead*

Lie number five - you may state that you are happy with what you have

Some individuals are happy with the level of success they have and they don't want or need their wealth to become greater than it is. Gratitude is a good thing to have and I am grateful for being alive. I believe that you are enough and should not take anything for granted.

I also know that it is nice to have more experiences, it's nice to be able to do more. It's nice to have protection and it's nice to prepare for those things you may not have dreamed about yet. When you do get that vision or dream, you are in great financial position to make it happen.

I also believe that God wants you to have and be more than what you are right now. In fact, I truly believe that you have been conditioned to do more, produce more and be creative but you can get stuck if you do not manage your resources properly, putting money aside allows you to do more than what you did yesterday.

Lie number six - you don't need to save because you may not live long enough to enjoy your wealth

The truth is you do not know how long you are going to live. What you do not want to happen is to live until the age of 79 without a good cash flow system. You need to be able to do the things you want to do at that age. People are living longer these days; My father died at the age of 89, and his older sister (my aunt) died at the age of 98. If you have a great network of people around you and a good cash flow system (which they did), then you'll age comfortably.

What is your reason for saving more money?

The reason for wanting to save more money must be clear in your mind. We all have our reasons and it's so important to have this written down and be reminded of it every day. Your why will lead you to your destiny and help you redefine who you are.

I never had a reason until I found myself seated in the staff car park holding on to my steering wheel, crying and shaking because my body did not want to go back to work. I had been bullied at work. I had been put on a Performance Improvement Plan (PIP) not once but twice; the second time it sparkled something inside of me.

Luckily enough one day, I built up the courage to go and sit in the staff canteen. This is where I overheard my co-workers talking about going to the Union representative because they had also been put on PIP, so I decided to do the same.

Whilst I was sitting down talking to the Union representative, my supervisor walked past. In fear, I quickly ran to my desk. He immediately came up to me and he said that I was no longer on a Performance Improvement Plan. That showed me that I had been bullied.

In that moment I also realised that I was financially unprepared. You see, I never had any savings for myself and I never had any savings for my daughter. I had allowed someone to have power over my livelihood.

Success was no longer about having a great job that paid well, it was about having options. This is my why, why I want to save more money so that I can have options.

What is your reason to save more money and how big is it? Is it big enough to drive you into action, to get you to want to make drastic changes in your life or do you need to find another reason that can drive you into action?

If your why is not big enough, you may stay stuck in the rat race or with those excuses and end up watching others become greater version of themselves.

If you want to save more money, then I urge you to consider using this system that I created in my financial empowerment programme. Make it authentic to you - it has to suit your lifestyle. So, that you can live the life you deserve for yourself and your family.

A life that encourages you and gives you the drive towards tremendous wealth and a healthier lifestyle. If you want more encouragement, then join our community. This is a new era, where you should look to not only save more money but become empowered, have renewed confidence, and live in abundance. I hope that you choose to be part of this new era so that you can fully embrace your full potential.

How to start saving ~ create a system

Motivational speaker Les Brown once said that '*There is no secret to success, you must learn a system. You must not be casual about your dreams; it will cause casualty... do the thing that others will not do...work on yourself... what is your strategy of being here?*'

Ramit Sethi also explained in his book *I will teach you to be rich*, that another way to save and be consistent is by '*...Going on the offensive by building a system that acknowledges our normal human behaviour. We can be distracted, and demotivated ... (it is therefore wise to) use tech to ensure that we are still growing our money.*'[42]

David Bach further stated that '*you need to have a system that doesn't depend on your following a budget or being disciplined.*'[43]

It's important to remember that building wealth can take time; it may take decades or a few years, but not days.

If you want it now, you will stay in need forever. However, if you wait for it to accumulate then you will have it for a lifetime.

David Bach insists that '*The one way to create lasting financial change that will help you build real wealth overtime is to ...MAKE YOUR FINANCIAL PLAN AUTOMATIC.*'[44]

---

42 R Sethi, 2020. *I Will Teach You To Be Rich*. 2nd Edition. London: Yellow Kite p 160

43 D Bach, 2004. *The Automatic millionaire — A Powerful one step plan to live and finish rich*. London: Penguin Group p 80

44 D Bach, 2004. *The Automatic millionaire — A Powerful one step plan to live and finish rich*. London: Penguin Group p 8

The system I created to help me save suits my lifestyle. I call this system the *empowerment system*. I hope by analysing my system, you can create your own system that suits you and gets you to your goals.

The empowerment system should work whether you're earning £4,000 or £250,000 per month. It should also work even if you win the lottery or get an inheritance.

> 66 *There is no secret to success, you must learn a system. You must not be casual about your dreams; it will cause casualty... do the thing that others will not do...work on yourself... what is your strategy of being here?*
>
> — *Les Brown*

The aim is to increase each percentage in each account (pot) every quarter until you get to the targeted amount.

You can make adjustments if the amount in the accounts is not increasing.

There are no limits as to how much you can earn and there are no limits to how much you can save.

However, there is a limit as to how much one can spend, you can only spend what is in the pot that month for that item.

This system helps you to manage God's money well and builds the kind of wealth others can only dream of.

The Empowerment system

First try and save at least 10% of your income after tax.

For example, if your income is £5,000 after tax, minus 10% and allocate it to your savings accounts which you should label with your why.

The why helps you to stick to your agenda.

£5,000 - 10% = £500 divide the sum total into 4 pots (£500 divide by 4) = £125.

Each savings account (pots) gets £125.

See below.

1. £125 towards - the opportunity account, one that can help generate more income.
2. £125 towards an ISA account until you reach the maximum allowance (for UK citizens). The maximum allowance is subject to change - check it every year.
3. £125 towards an asset that will generate an income.
4. £125 for any income loss - aim to save at least three months income (minimum) or up to 12 months (maximum).

This equals £500 saved per month.

You can also gain interest if you use bank accounts that pay interest.

After you have reached your maximum with your ISA you can then start investing the £125 into stocks and shares.

This will generate even more income in the future. Please see *Power in Investment* in chapter five for more information about ISAs.

To increase your savings, you should aim to increase your income every quarter by either earning more or cutting down expenses.

Points to note:

1. Each account should have the minimum and maximum percentage amount allocated to them. It can be from as little as 1% for the first quarter of the month. Start with an amount that you are comfortable with.

2. You then have to drip feed into those accounts by using direct debit or standing order until you reach your maximum target. Let the accounts be open to receive.

3. You have to work on your money blocks constantly and the only way to do this is to have an accountability partner or community. When one person wins, then you all win and learn to share ideas on how to get to the next level. The partner has to encourage your money to grow and not have fancy ideas on how to spend it or how it can help them.

4. Remember once you set up the system try and get it out of sight and out of mind. You can review the accounts per quarter.

5. The main account where transactions come from should be reviewed daily to check for any inaccuracies. Try and grow a buffer for at least one month's income. This buffer will be your new zero in your main account. This should act as your overdraft.

6. Ensure that the accounts are separate from each other. For example, pot one the opportunity account can be with HSBC Bank and pot number two the ISA account can be with Vanguard. This makes it harder for you to touch your savings.

7. Think of the whole system as a muscle or a business you are growing and be focused. Once you have built the muscle for each account, you can get on with your life and never have to worry about money or the lack thereof.

If you make any errors do not worry ~ just readjust your account until you get it right

Ramit Sethi states that you should follow this ratio:
- 50% for essential bills
- 10% for savings
- 20% -30% for fun money

I say try:
- 50% for essentials
- 10% savings
- 20% daily expenses
- 20% (entertainment)

If you pay tithes to your church, you can take 10% of your entertainment money to use. If you are giving to charities, such as churches you can donate the money through Gift Aid. This means these charities including churches can claim an extra 25p for every £1 you give (in the UK).

Essential and daily expenses

Some internet banks such as Monese will also allow you to save in pots for different situations.

This will allow you to allocate your spending money according to those situations that help your home to function.

For example, you can have several pots for you daily expenses. In this case 20% of £5000 which is £1000.

£1000 divided by 10 pots:

1. Pot for medicine/health
2. Pot for your child's school uniform, school outings and childcare/tuition fees
3. Pot for clothing allowances
4. Pot for car maintenance before insurance kicks in
5. Pot for Christmas
6. Pot for birthdays
7. Pot for holidays
8. Pot for business ventures
9. Pot for household products
10. Pot for hair products and maintenance

You can increase your pots if you find that you have something you regularly pay for that you want to include:

Please remember you can start off with a small amount in each pot and increase it every quarter when your income increases.

50% for the essential bills will be £2,500.

Essential bills:

1. Food
2. Gas
3. Electric
4. Rent/mortgage payment
5. Council tax
6. Water bill
7. Travel
8. Internet/phone bill
9. Insurance
10. Loans

20% entertainment money is £1000 from a £5000 income:

1. Swimming lessons
2. Dance classes
3. Parties
4. Theatre trips or movies
5. Books
6. Restaurants, eating out and takeaway

When your entertainment money is gone, it's gone. You can't take out the money in your savings account to pay for entertainment.

Other schemes

When I started my saving journey, I entered a savings scheme called **a pardner.**

I was introduced to a pardner scheme (some call it susu) by a friend. She said that this was how she could afford her holidays and other luxuries, and all I had to do was commit to £20 a week or whatever I could afford.

Her friend was the leading person whom I did not know, which made this very risky for me. I had heard about the pardner scheme through relatives, but I never participated.

It is where you give in a regular sum of money weekly into a group or monthly. Each week or month, one group member gets the complete sum of cash. The member still has to continue to put in the weekly sum of money.

You all take it in turn to withdraw the money collected each week or each month. This continues on until you pull out of the scheme so you must inform the members.

It has its advantages because you have accountability partners, and you are accountable to others.

It also feels good to have a large sum of cash after those months or weeks of putting the money away. It allows you to be able to afford luxuries without having to borrow from a bank.

You put into it, what you can afford to put in consistently.

The disadvantage of that system is that you have to have a lot of trust that the members will pay in the amount each week or month, because some members default on their payments.

If anything happens to the person holding on to the money, you might have a problem getting your money back as it's not regulated by the Financial Conduct Authority (FCA).

Another disadvantage I found was that if close family members are involved, they may start dictating to you how you should spend your cash and how you should be able to lend them money because you have X amount coming in.

It can be rewarding but also risky and you do not get paid any interest, as you would do with a bank.

I believe that there are some apps and companies that are running similar schemes in the U.K.

Many people have saved up their deposits to buy houses because of those schemes.

In summary, when you enter such schemes, you must have:

- A savings goal
- Ask questions at the beginning
- Have membership meetings quarterly so that everyone is aware of the rules
- Build momentum because it's not easy for everyone involved
- Have set rules written down as to how the group would manage if certain situations occurred

Making sacrifices (saving aggressively)

In order to save aggressively, you might need to make a few sacrifices such as downsizing or moving in with other people to share the rent and bills. I am aware that not everyone is in the position to make those sacrifices.

When you are trying to save money, do not compromise your well-being. You can lose your money and get it back if your mind is in the right place but if your mind is not right then the chances of you getting that money might be slim.

> 66 *Saving money is a marathon not a race - It takes commitment.*

Affirm that: **money works in my favour, if I make the wrong decision I learn from my errors and if I make the right decisions I am rewarded for my efforts.**

Every time you are about to spend the money in your savings accounts, you should ask yourself one question. If you spent this money, would the purchase bring you closer to your goals or hinder you from taking advantage of better opportunities?

Once you have answered the question, sleep on it until the next day, then reach out to your accountability partner for a second opinion. After that, decide whether or not to make the purchase because after all, it's you that has to live with the consequences of your decisions.

66 *When you are trying to save money, do not compromise your well-being*

CHAPTER 5

Empower in Investments

" *You want the knowledge and discipline to be able to make decisions on your own* "

— *Sandra Kaima*

E mpower in Investment is an extensive topic, and I believe that you need to read about it in various books and invest in courses that cover the ins and out of investment so that you can get the correct investment information.

I would urge you to sign up for the "Super Simple Investing" course and learn about investing at *https://sky08-financialjoyacademy.thrivecart.com/super-simple-investing/*

The course has given me better knowledge and understanding of how to invest my money correctly.

The "Super Simple Investing" course is worth doing even after you have read all the books.

The calculations on the course are an eye-opener. They allow you to plan for the future.

The course includes the seven ways you could invest your money if you do not invest in stocks and shares.

The course highlights the definitions of the symbols and goes through different investment platforms so you can visualise how to invest step by step.

You can compare your investment accounts as you go along and make any investment changes to boost your investment (this is what I did).

The course will give you more clarity and confidence. The knowledge I gained from doing the course helped me be a better investor.

One thing you should be aware of is that if you take on high risk, you may get high rewards, but you could also lose your money. Your risk appetite depends on your age and circumstances.

Why should you invest your money?

- Investing your money in shares and bonds and other commodities such as property is another way of creating passive income. Your money works for you without you having to leave your bed.
- You own a share of a company's equity, which means that you are indirectly a business owner, and if your portfolio is diverse, it means that you can own shares in lots of different companies globally (imagine owning a piece of the company in the USA without you having to step out of your house in the UK).
- The value of your money stays up most of the time, which means you can beat inflation. If your money

is sitting in the bank earning no interest. It loses its value.

Example of inflation

The price of bread might have been 35 pence in 1990, and now it is £1. Therefore, you would get less for your money.

Investing your money allows you to beat inflation because you expect to get more in return for your money.

- Inflation is said to go up at least 2.5 per cent every year, which means that your money can lose its value that much faster. When you invest your money, you could get returns of over 5-8% or more over some time (5 to 10 years). (Provided that you have allocated your assets in the right places).
- You could live on the interest alone if you invest your money earlier, like in your 20's or if you invest a considerable amount of money in shares and stocks that yield high returns. You could use the money for your expenses, such as that trip to Dubai or Hawaii. The returns can also pay for private education for your children, fly first class or buy multiple homes. (Anything is possible).

True story

A friend once told me that his uncle asked him to invest his money at a young age (although he had no idea why). He now lives on the returns whilst his money (the principal amount that he invested) this still invested and earning more interest. He never has to work for anyone else to receive that money because, essentially, his money is now working for him, putting himself at an advantage.

Another example

For instance, if my 21-year daughter invested £600 a month (the money she earns whilst she is still living at home) for the next ten years and received interest of 7% rate of return on average. She could receive around £102,631.04 after ten years with compounding by the time she is 31 years old. She would be left to leave on purpose for a purpose. (I hope she is reading this).

It is also great to find a tax-sufficient way of investing. If you live in the UK or the USA, products such as ISA have a tax allowance which means that you do not have to pay capital gains tax on that amount—encouraging you to save even more money.

You can also get paid dividend; this is extra money for you. Dividends is a share of the company's profit. Company directors decide whether to pay out dividends to its shareholders or to reinvest the money back into the company.

Disadvantage of investing

- Environmental factors such as the war or a crisis can cause the market values to go up and down affecting your investments.

- You will be charged fees for investing on platforms. This could eat into your investments.
- Companies can go bust, but this could be mitigated if you invest in a diverse market, i.e. not put all your eggs in one basket.
- Ordinary individuals such as you and I do not usually invest directly in companies on the stock market because this is a very high-risk investment, and we could lose our money very quickly if that particular company goes bust or its shares plummet for some reason. Companies, banks, and the super-rich are much more likely to invest in individual companies because they can afford to take on much higher-risk investments.

How do you invest?

Before you invest, you may want to ask yourself a few questions such as:

- What is your goal for now and shortly for your money – how much money would you like to earn by away of investment, and for what reason? For example, would you like to be free of financial worries or to go on multiple holidays, retire early, or just be able to spend on luxuries without worrying about money.
- Are you going to invest long-term or short-term? Would you take much more significant risks and do daily trading? And if you're taking the long-term

view, how much do you expect to gain at the end of
the 5, 10 or 20-year period?

- What market are you going to invest in? For example,
is it the UK market or the USA market etc.
- Decide what platform you will invest on, for example,
Vanguard, Hargreaves Lansdown or iShares.
- You will then have to decide what funds you would
like to invest in, ETF or Index Fund or have it done for
you. Strategies like the life strategies with Vanguard,
which have a mixture of bonds and shares.
- How much risk are you willing to take? for example,
you could decide to invest 100% in shares only or you
could decide to mitigate your risk and invest 50% in
shares and 50% in bonds.

Index Funds, ETFs, and Bonds

What is an index / Index fund / ETF?

Indexes are a group of companies that combine to make up
the index. The index is a portfolio of diverse companies,
such as oil or technology companies. An example of an
index company is FTSE 100. In the UK, FTSE 100 has 100
of the best companies. S&P 500 in the USA has over 500
of the best companies.

An index fund is a fund that investors have put money
in collectively to invest in the index. When you invest in
an index fund, you spread the risk because you get to put
your money in different companies that make up the index.
If Company A does badly and Company B does good, your

losses (invested cash) can be minimised. At one end, you will lose some of the money you have invested, but at the other end, you may gain and make a profit on the money you have invested, making you a winner.

Your returns may not be as profitable as they may have been if you had invested in individual stocks. However, you are almost guaranteed some returns over a long period. Some investors fear losing money when they invest. The index funds ensure that the risk can be mitigated by diversification; the only way you could lose money is if all companies went bust on the stock exchange, which is not likely to happen.

ETFs are called Exchange-traded funds – they are listed on the stock exchange index funds are not listed on the stock exchange. ETF's can be diversified, and fees are typically a little more than index funds, you could invest in both ETF's and Index funds for diversification.

ETFs have no minimum requirement as to how much you have to pay to invest in them, making investment accessible to ordinary people like me and you to invest.

Bonds

You can invest in Bonds in the UK or USA market.

Bonds come in different forms. The main difference between bonds and shares is that bonds may offer you a fixed interest rate on your investment as a promise that you will get the principal amount that you invested returned to you.

Bonds are a lower-risk investment, and you may not get high returns, but at least you will have a much-increased chance of getting the principal (the money you borrowed from the government or companies) back.

It is recommended that the older you get, the fewer risks you may want to take. For example, Vanguard may offer you a strategic structure that gives you, 60% shares and 40% in bonds, which reduces your risks.

There are different types of investment products you can invest in the UK:

1. ISA- tax efficient - cash ISA, stocks and shares, SIPP etc
2. Bonds- Lower-risk or high-risk bonds
3. Stocks/shares – can be High risk
4. Cash – does not beat inflation.
5. REITS- real estate investment

Index funds and ETFs make it easier and possible for us to reach our financial freedom due to their low fees and low-cost price to get in.

You can also invest in commodities like gold, paintings, and cryptocurrency; however, you must do your research and be aware of how much risk you are taking.

You can start investing your money using a small amount of money according to the percentage the brokers want.

Some platforms will allow you to invest in as little as £25, allowing you to drip-feed your investment, but their fees could also be higher.

Investing in individual stocks

Individual stocks are riskier because you rely on that company alone to make a profit. If it does not make a profit, you could lose your money if the company goes bust for whatever reason.

When that individual company does exceptionally well, you could also earn much bigger profits.

Warren Buffett, the world's best-known investor in the world has a net worth of over $108 billion as of 2023.

He made a bet that index funds that were unmanaged by Vanguard would outperform Hedge funds that were managed by Fund managers who charged a high fee for their expertise over ten years.

The index fund outperformed the managed Hedge funds. He stated that only a few Hedge fund managers can pick out the best-performing stocks.

Therefore, arguably index funds are favoured in most cases to get a better return for your money over ten years. A few reasons why it can be considered prudential to invest in index funds are:

1. You do not have to do anything other than put in your money, and the computer algorithm chooses what funds the investment is spread into.
2. The fees are much lower.
3. Your investment is diversified, meaning the risk is spread over various companies.

Power of compounding

A company can give its shareholders interest on a daily, monthly, or yearly bases.

Compounding interest is interest (I)calculated on the initial principal (IP). It includes the accumulated interest. (AI) from the first year.

For example

If interest gained annually was 10%

£100 x 10% = £10

£100(IP) + £10 (AI) = £110

As a result of the second year, you would have got.

£110 x 10% (I) calculated annually = £11 the interest gained IG)

(£110 (IP + AI) + £11 (IG) = £121

Your money grows more when the interest rate goes up. Say, for example, from 10% to 12%.

£121 x 12% = £14.52

£121 + £14.52 = £135.52

Money gained on interest on top of interest is known as compounding interest.

To illustrate the point even further.

If you had £10,000 invested x 10% interest paid annually, you would gain = £1,000 each year or more if interest rates increase.

This is another form of passive income (money you have earned at the end of the year without working for it). which you can use it to reinvest or spend as you please. This is subject to any tax implications.

Is investment only for the rich?

Investment in index funds and ETFs has made it possible for those not yet super rich to invest in the stock market without taking on high risk.

If you are super rich (Amen!), it may be wise to get a financial advisor that can help you diversify your portfolio to get much higher returns.

I recommend you check out the following book and articles to move you closer to the investment world.

- Tony Robbins Money: Master the Game and Unshakeable your financial freedom and playbook – creating peace of mind in a world of volatility with Peter Mallouk
  - Check out articles on the *thehumblepenny.com/pay-off-debts-fast-or-invest*
- If you want to know more, I highly recommend this course, Super Simple Investment. Click here for *https://sky08--financialjoyacademy.thrivecart.com/super-simple-investing* [45]

Don't let a lack of knowledge keep you from getting ahead.

In the words of Les Brown "it isn't enough to be casual about your dreams".

---

45 affiliate link

Advantages of investing earlier

The earlier you invest your money, the more returns you can get in the future. For example, let's look at a person who invests in their 20s compared to the person who invests in their 40s.

The return on investments at 20 years old is greater, which means that the longer you invest your money, the more money you will make on top of the money you have invested. If you have passed the age of 40, you should not be put off by this because a return is better than no return at all. When you invest earlier, you are much more likely to manage the turmoil and bumps in the road without fear of losing your money. Older investors will also benefit from investing but they would need to start now.

Fear of failure

Fear of failing is a block that can lead to anxiety and distress over time. It can manifest itself into mental health issues and as a result, eventually cause you to become depressed.

When it comes to investment it is well known that 'past performance is no indicator of future success.' You will see this notice time and time again when you are about to invest your money or throughout any research on investments.

This means that there is no guarantee that you will get your money back and let's be honest, nobody wants to fail. You may not want to fail which is very understandable. However, sometimes you can fail to give yourself a chance to win and therefore, not bother to invest at all.

If you are going to get into the investment game, then you must be okay with losing some money. The capacity to let it go and move on is the attitude you need because the markets are sometimes unpredictable.

In *Rich Dad Poor Dad*, Robert Kiyosaki stated that '*Everyone has the fear of losing money; the difference is how you handle fear and losing. The primary difference between a rich person and a poor person is how they manage that fear.*'[46]

He also goes on to state that '*Texans don't bury their failures. They get inspired by them. They take their failures and turn them into rallying cries. Failures inspire Texans to become winners... It is a formula for all winners.*'[47]

It must be said that not being afraid to lose money can be mentally challenging for many people. I recall a time when I lost £1,000 from a fraudster who promised great returns for my money.

> **Fear of failing is a block that can lead to anxiety and distress over time.**

When he asked for more, I knew then and there that this was a prank. I kindly backed off and it hurt because

---

46 Kiyosaki, R T. 2017. Rich Dad Poor Dad, 3rd Edition – 20th Anniversary edition, United Stated of America: Plata Publisher. LLC p 205

47 Kiyosaki, R T. 2017. Rich Dad Poor Dad, 3rd Edition – 20th Anniversary edition, United Stated of America: Plata Publisher. LLC p 208

I knew that I would not get that money back. I had learnt never to make the same mistake again and my consolation was that he will not be getting any more than that. I had to learn from my mistake and move on, turning my failure into a new opportunity.

I turned my losses into wins because I decided to do my own research on how to invest money, rather than try to take the easy way out.

I walked away with a loss but along with it came wisdom that costed me £1000. I knew that I could make back the £1000 or even more, because I was still here. I had faith that I could make more money in the long run; there is a greater possibility of earning a million if you are still alive. The £1000 did not take me out, it highlighted the fact that I had to be very careful with how I invested my money. There are people out there who lose millions every day and give up on life. If you are one of them, I want you to know that mistakes happen, but you must learn from them and make wiser choices next time.

Listening to what people say

There are people who have gone into the investment game without doing their research and have lost. As a result, they vowed to never invest their money in the stock market again.

A friend of mine did just that, he invested $75,000. He never saw a return on that money and when I asked him how he invested his money, it turned out that his investment was in individual stocks that promised him a high return. He took on a much higher risk.

This could have easily deterred me from investing, but I decided to read a few books on investment, and I also carried out my own research. My friend was deeply hurt, which resulted in him walking away without analysing his mistakes or lack of knowledge. Reading books such as *I can make you rich*[48] can give you foundation knowledge on how you can start investing your money and how to reduce your losses.

Habits

The one thing that I found to be true is that we live in a world of instant gratification; we want everything now and not tomorrow. Investing your money for the long term means that you may not get results tomorrow. You may have to wait a decade to see results, and this is a challenge for most of us.

If you get into the habit of investing which demands that you think ahead and recondition your mindset, you will undoubtedly be on your way to real wealth. To do this, you should start with perhaps investing in small chunks and as your mind gets stronger, you should increase that amount gradually. You must remember that an investment is a long-term strategy. It can incur losses which you have to be able to mitigate without losing yourself.

You should carry out your own research to become familiar with financial terms and have an awareness on

---

48 R Sethi, 2020. *I Will Teach You To Be Rich*. 2nd Edition. London: Yellow Kite

how the economy is moving. This means that every now and again, you should buy financial journals or papers like the Financial Times and network with like-minded people so you can gain more knowledge. It is important to start educating yourself and being aware, even if you have not started to invest your money. You never know which side the windfall may come from.

If you happen to get paid or receive a million pounds today, would you know what to do with it? How would you invest that money today? You cannot start carrying out your research the day the money goes into your account. This is because research takes time, and it is much better to be in a position whereby you have the information you need to make the right choices before someone comes along and makes them for you.

Seek wisdom today and be ready to use it tomorrow.

Before you make any decision, you must study the consequences of it. A decision is easy to make but living with the consequences can be much harder. You must learn to fall gracefully and get up if you make the wrong decisions.

When I decided to leave my council property for a chance to get on the property ladder, the decision was easy to make because I had analysed the consequences beforehand.

I sat down almost every evening and made a few notes. I worked out the worst-case scenario for me - losing my income without having accomplished what I had set out to do, which was to buy a house.

However, I realised that even with the possible losses, I could still save money even if I ended up back on welfare. I also knew that the flat I was holding on to, took up most of my wages and the high rising bills did not help my situation. It still worked out that financially, I was better off living with my parents.

I took into consideration a few more things, such as:

If I bought the house and lost my job, I could rent it until I found another job or share it with someone who will help me pay the mortgage. You are not allowed to rent out a council property because the flat is technically the council's, not yours.

I spoke to different people that had bought homes and I read a few newspapers. I also went onto the Money Saving Expert website to get as much information as possible. I listened and saw how people moved with their finances and then made the decision because after all, time was not on my side. I was soon turning 40, I had spoken to a friend who said that the banks consider your age when you're buying a home. I felt like time was against me at that point. It was either I do it or don't.

What would happen if you decided to take that chance and give up what you have now in order to change your future and generations to come?

Whatever decision you make always boils down to whether you can live with the consequences if things do not work out as planned. It is also wise to consider how long you can withstand the storm, because life happens and our resilience will always be tested.

Buying a home to me is a bit similar to investing your money in stocks whether we choose to do it by index fund or invest in individual stocks. There is a chance that you could win big but there is also a chance that you could lose. Either way, you will still live to tell the tale and work on improving yourself and others. It is wise to always prepare for new opportunities.

For myself, I would rather tell the tale of the time that I tried instead of a story of many regrets.

Is investing gambling?

About 20 years ago, I read in the newspaper about the Church of England investing in an oil company. I believe the reason why this particular story was in the newspaper, was because the oil had got into the sea which killed a lot of animals.

The story was mainly about the ethical ground of the church and the companies they had chosen to invest in. What took me by surprise was that the church was investigating its money. It made me realise that investing cannot be a bad thing to do if the church was doing it. Is it immoral or gambling? I suppose it depends on how you look at it. If you have no money to invest and you are taking chances with the money, then in my opinion, you're gambling. You may also want to look at the companies you're investing in and ask yourself whether these companies are ethical by your standards.

To help you be able to make better decisions as to whether you are ready to invest, you should consider a few things:

1. Do you have an emergency fund set aside for at least three to six months that would help you manage if there was a possible loss of income?
2. Have you paid off your mortgage or do you have a plan to pay it off?
3. Have you paid off your debts or have a plan to pay them off?
4. Do you have spare cash to put aside for the long run and other opportunities?

This parable shows that investing whether it is in wealth or the gifts that you have been given is not a bad thing, but rather an honourable thing to do.

In Matthew 25:14–30, the parable of the talents tells us about a master who was leaving his house to travel, and before leaving, entrusted his property to his servants. According to the abilities of each man, one servant received five talents, the second had received two, and the third received only one. The property entrusted to the three servants was worth eight talents, where a talent was a significant amount of money. Upon returning home after a long absence, the master asks his three servants for an account of the talents he entrusted to them. The first and the second servants explained that they each put their talents to work and have doubled the value of the property. Each servant was rewarded.

Matthew 25:23: The Lord said unto him: Well done, good and faithful servant; thou hast been faithful over a few things, I will make thee ruler over many things. Enter thou into the joy of thy Lord.

The third servant, however, had hidden his talent, burying it in the ground and was punished by his master:

Matthew 25:24-30: Then he which had received the one talent came that hath not shall be taken away even that which he hath. And cast ye the unprofitable servant into outer darkness: there shall be weeping and gnashing of teeth.[49]

geneva.edu/blog/everyday-living/cultivating-gods-blessings quotes that:

- We must put our talents into action.
- We will be granted exactly what we need to fulfil God's bidding.
- We will eventually be held accountable if we do not put our talents into action - we have to remember that.

If you are unable to invest in yourself due to circumstances beyond your control, you should still try and gain as much knowledge as you can about investing and then pass it down to the next generation so that they can make informed decisions.

---

49 Wikipedia, 2022, Parable of the talents or minas [website] Available: [Accessed 5 December 2022] *en.wikipedia.org/wiki/Parable_of_the_talents_or_minas#:~:text=According%20to%20the%20abilities%20of,a%20significant%20amount%20of%20money*

Money is a tool that helps you enjoy life. However, your health will always come first and with good health, you can be happy even with the little money you have. Whatever you decide to do, make sure that you put your health first.

CHAPTER 6

Empower in Giving

❝ *You cannot give from an empty pot* **❞**

— *Sandra Kaima*

Giving from your harvest offers you the opportunity to give back to those in need at that time. If you are out there giving from an empty hand, or an empty pot (if you do not have any money to give, and then, you give your last coins away). You have now made yourself vulnerable and weak and are no longer able to give because you have given from a place of lack, whether its love or something else. If you have not got it, you simply haven't got it.

I am not suggesting that you should not give or do things for free, but you should not be so gullible in believing that you must offer your services for free all the time. Free is wonderful but so is getting paid so you can meet your basic needs.

It's very impractical to give away your gifts and talents for free and then beg someone else for money. Your freeness will have you being homeless where your talents would soon perish because you are not living in a suitable environment for your abilities to be nourished.

Have you ever seen anyone cheering on a singer who is not making much money?

People cheer singers who make millions. There are plenty of Beyoncé's out there, but they are not making the money that she is. This amount of money puts her in a position whereby she can afford to give. Regarding charity events, people tend to gravitate towards the one who has more money to give.

If you want to give, you have to learn how to create the kind of money you would like to give to others or good causes. These should be causes that support people and make the world a better place to live. Therefore, the more money you make, the more you can give and make a change.

If you are going to give, you should give a percentage of what you can afford to give at the time. It will:

1. Help you get into the habit of giving.
2. Awaken the spirit of gratitude, which is excellent for your wellbeing. For instance, you can say that you are so grateful for what you have, that you can afford to give to others who need it more.
3. It's also a nice feeling to give - it uplifts others and supports good causes so that the next generation can be happier than before.

Give wisely, not just to anyone or anything. Also, be conscious and weary of whom or what you're giving to because at times you may do more damage and have more regrets.

As for everything in life, you must look at your decisions and the consequences. Are you feeding a bad habit or are you being supportive? Are you patronising? Is it better to give a person or group of people tools and knowledge to feed themselves rather than giving them money? Is it better to give to a person (or people) knowledge and tool to feed themselves, or is it better to give them money?

I recall a time in my life when I gave my money to anyone begging on the streets of London. During this time, I had student loans, credit card debt and no income.

Whilst living in Newham, I would often run to the petrol station in the middle of the night to get my electricity charged. I always saw this guy asking for money while sitting next to the ATM. I automatically took out my last coins and gave them to him.

I would then go home and wake up the next day, asking myself how on earth I would pay back the bank loans and all the debts I had accumulated over the years whilst studying.

Nobody seemed to be hiring and I kept getting rejection letters (this was happening even before the 2008 recession).

On a Monday morning, on my way to sign on at the job centre, I saw the same guy who sat at the ATM machine those nights that I went to the petrol station to charge my key. This guy was now wearing a clean suit, and in his hands, he was counting the cash he was holding. They were not small coins - it was a bundle of notes with the late Queen's face smiling at him. We crossed the road on opposite sides.

My eyes stared at him whilst he was grinning; he did not recognise me because he was too busy counting the cash in his hands.

He continued to sit at the ATM as usual, but this was the last time I gave money to a guy begging on the streets. You see, I figured it out that pretending to be homeless and begging was an occupation for some. They had not one but two non-taxable incomes: the benefit money and the cash they accumulated waiting at ATMs.

They knew suckers like me would eventually pour out their last coins. Every penny counts. It did for him, and it should for you.

He continued to sit outside the ATM, and I continued to get my electric and gas keys charged at the machine. But on these occasions, my coins stayed in my pockets. This incident disturbed me for months. I was bewildered and jealous that I was not the one holding that stack of cash.

> 66 *As for everything in life, you must look at your decisions and the consequences*

A time to give

Okay it was not the last time I gave someone money. Let's be honest, a giver is a giver and if it is in you, it's in you.

Years later, I had moved out of Canning Town and into my savings journey. I bought my first home and I was still driving my mum's car which took me from A- Z.

I had walked inside the petrol station shop to pay for my petrol as I lined up in the queue. In front of me was a gentleman who seemed to be trembling, in a suit. He took out his credit cards one by one and each was declined; it looked like the shopkeeper was giving him a hard time.

I stepped in and asked what was wrong. The shopkeeper asked me whether I was going to help him pay for the petrol with an attitude. I answered confidently asking how much the petrol was and when the shopkeeper said it was £25, I said I would pay for it. The shopkeeper raised his neck to look at me even because he was taken back by my response. He then told the guy that it was okay and that he could pay later.

The shopkeeper never took the money from me, but he did ask me why I offered to pay. I told him that I could see that the guy was trembling.

What astonished me the most was that he was driving a really expensive car and looked good in flashy clothes but was not able to pay for his petrol.

It made me reflect on myself and encouraged me to continue driving my not-so-good car until I could afford to buy a new one. It was important for me to continue my savings journey and top up my emergencies.

The truth is that you would never know which way the tables might turn. You may need to be given the resources to support you, or you may find yourself in a better position to give. Managing your resources whether small or big is vital to a prosperous life.

Habits again

You give according to your formal experiences and what you have been accustomed to. My father used to take me to church and he would often give me and my sisters £1 coins to give during offering. That was want I was accustomed to, so when I got older and was able take myself to church, I continued giving £1.

When I went to other churches, I saw that giving was a massive part of the services especially in Protestant churches. People would write out cheques and take out their credit cards. Admittedly, I was shocked and mesmerised and I did not understand how people could give so freely without a second thought. So, I increased my coins to £2.

It took one night of partying and drinking to show me how easily I could spend £50 on drinks that made me feel sick the next day. I thought if I could spend so much on partying, which did nothing for my spirit or to prepare me for life, why was I so tight with giving to God's church? A place that fed me the word of God, which greatly impacted my confidence for the entire week and taught me to navigate the world positively.

I started to see that giving to church was not only for my soul, but a way of saying thank you and ensuring that the church could serve its people and pay its bills.

So that we could all worship in a warm environment allowing us to focus on prayer and connection with God.

What is your experience in giving? Are you a reluctant giver?

When I lived in Newham, I visited the Catholic church and I recall this tall white priest saying that he felt uncomfortable asking folks for money, but the church needed it. The old heating system needed repairing and I was at that church for a good 10 years, but they were still raising money for the heating system.

I compared this to other Christian churches who were not afraid to ask; they made it a must. The Catholic priest most certainly may have to borrow some of other churches tactics to get people to do the right thing for themselves without feeling guilty. People should feel encouraged to give - it is the right thing to do for both the congregation and the community.

Special occasions

Still in Newham, a good friend of mine who was a practising Jehovah Witness, would come to my house with her daughter and we would go through the Bible. My first child was turning seven and I was preparing for her birthday party. I had invited people and I was trying to put everything together.

A few days before the birthday party, my friend came to visit me with her two daughters and she told us that Jehovah Witnesses do not celebrate birthdays or Christmas. I was shocked. She added that they give each other presents throughout the year to show appreciation.

After hearing this, I told her I was too busy to have any more meetings and we never had a prayer meeting again.

Once the party was done, I could not help but consider how much money they saved by not participating in these traditions. How stress-free their lives must be without having to have the heavy burden of always thinking of a birthday present or a Christmas gift.

When it comes to Christmas, birthdays and even valentine's day, you may like to receive presents and it's just as nice to be able to give gifts as well.

You may sometimes feel unwanted, perhaps unappreciated, and emotional, if no one has given you a present or a card on your birthday. You may have it in mind that you have to receive to know that you're loved, when in fact this is not true. Nobody should feel obligated to give you a present to show how much they love you. A simple hug or the person's presence in your life alone should make you feel and know that you're loved.

The problem is not the giving because it is nice to give, the problem comes when you are made to feel obligated to give, even when you cannot afford to.

The pain often comes because you did not create an account for those special moments. You know that you have birthdays that you would like to celebrate, you know that Christmas is a special time that you would like to also celebrate which comes along every year on the same day. You know that Mother's Day, Father's Day and even valentine's day will soon be coming up. If you incorporate a giving account in your financial plans or system that caters for those special occasions, it will make your life and managing your finances much easier.

Have you set aside any cash for Christmas this year and if not ask yourself why? What is blocking you from setting aside that money?

The lack of financial preparation can lead to you feeling depressed too, and you may get the blues after the Christmas holiday. It normally occurs when you have borrowed money or spent your last wages on buying presents that you did not plan for.

You could end up entering the new year in debt or pulling your money from each bank account to make up the extra cash you have spent. Some people also have low mood swings, coming from the hype and excitement of Christmas to a huge realisation that it was just that. A big hype and nothing more. Many forget the true essence of Christmas which is to celebrate the birth of Jesus.

Anxiety and headaches kick in, from the thought of having to pay back the money you may have borrowed. It's almost like a trap most fall into year, after year.

My only suggestion is that you open up a separate account for Christmas, birthdays and other special occasions and drip feed your money into those accounts, little by little. This would make a huge difference and meet all your expectations without stress because it will be in alignment with what you can afford to do.

It is essential to set boundaries regarding how much you should spend on giving. Giving is a good thing to do - it's a mark of celebration of one's life, together with your children or a loved one.

However, you should never think that you are not loved enough, if you are not given any presents. Fearing what might happen if so and so does not get that present and the ugly repercussions that may haunt you is all in your head. The truth is you cannot love someone any more or less than the present they have not yet received. It is practically impossible.

After opening a separate giving account and putting aside what you can afford monthly, you should stick to the spending budget for each person or event and get on with the rest of your life.

Relinquish the power of people pleasing because this is what you are doing when you give people things you cannot afford. Giving stuff you cannot afford will make you unhappy, broke, in debt and further away from having freedom of choice.

Can you remember what your friends or relatives gave you last year for Christmas or two years ago for Christmas?

Ask a friend or a family member if they remember the presents you gave them last year and see how long they take to answer that question. If they don't remember, don't worry because this is normal.

However, if you ask your family or friends about the last time you made them happy, they will tell you about an experience or a moment they spent with you. Our experiences with others are much more valuable than wrapped up presents or money.

That person or child you are giving or planning to give a costly present to will not remember it either.

Living in the moment and not in the future ahead of you, will always get you stuck and wondering why things are not changing. Why is your money not growing?

Giving to those who ask

It is natural to feel uncomfortable whenever you lend money to someone, and they fail to give it back. All sorts of negative thoughts may spring up about that person when you least expect it and your opinion of that person may change.

One of my friend's father, Uncle Albert, said to me at the age of 15, that if you're going to lend money to a friend, you might as well forget about your money and friendship. What he meant was that, if you really want to give your friend money, give it to them and do not expect the money back, because it will kill your friendship if they do not give it back to you.

Creating multiple families

One of the things that some partners do in their relationship is trap themselves by having multiple families outside here and there. With multiple families, whatever money the partner is getting must be divided between themselves and their many wives or husbands and children. Therefore, they end up giving continuously giving money away. Practising monogamy may not be such a bad idea; after all, it keeps your expenses down.

For example George, might have two children with Mary whom he shares his income with in the same household.

Years later George has an affair with Crystal and this results in a child and now he has to split his income between two households.

Giving to extended family

Some people keep on giving their relatives abroad money, on a regular basis. In fact, most of the phone calls they get are not about their wellbeing. They will probably contain stories about a relative back home being in hospital or about lack of school fees for someone. Instead of the person being focused on their purpose and serving more, they end up working two or three jobs to provide for others abroad. They end up working much harder and living an impoverished lifestyle to help and support their friends and extended families. At times, they may feel obligated to support and for some reason they create this idea in their minds that those abroad are living in unfortunate situations.

It is wise to encourage those relatives back home to learn to earn their own money. You can do this by supporting them to set up a business or to help them find work which can help them meet their own needs for life. You need to ask yourself this question: how long would those relatives survive without you giving them money? Remember, there is a beginning and an end to everything.

Giving to the poor

We are often taught that we must give to the poor, however, what is defined as poor? Rabbi Daniel states that we should:

'*...Give to those in need that you have the power to help. But do not believe there is some well-defined class of poor you are obligated to support. When you do help in this way, you help not only the receipts of charity, but you also help yourself by bolstering your morals and sense of self-worth, which will, in turn, improve the way others see you.*'[50]

Give and you shall receive

Personally, I love giving whether it is my time or my advice. If my heart is speaking to me to give and I can afford it, I will give.

I personally do not give to charities to receive, however, after reading Rabbi Lapin's statement, it made me realise a few things about what I do get in return or what I have received in return indirectly.

Every time I give and make another person smile, I get fulfilment and joy, which makes me feel complete.

An example of this is the time when I decided to run the half-marathon, for Great Ormond Street hospital. Ironically, a few years later, my first child got treatment at that same hospital. Now, that was one hell of a coincidence.

---

50 Rabbi Lapin, D., 2014. Business Secrets From The Bible - Spiritual Success Strategies For Financial Abundance, New Jersey / Canada: Wiley p. 242

You should never give to receive

If you intentionally give to receive, you will end up walking around annoyed with yourself if you do not get anything back in return. If you catch anyone sulking or yourself moaning, then that was false giving. You will end up feeling drained and empty because you gave with expectations and not from your heart. Be a genuine giver.

David Bach, states that:

> *'The more you give, the wealthier you feel...money often flows faster to those who give because givers attract abundance into their lives rather than scarcity.'*[51]

He sets out the things you should consider before giving. To become an automatic giver, he stated that you must, decide on how much you want to give, choose a charity you care about and trust and automate your charitable donations on a monthly or biweekly basis. Keep a track of your donations for tax purposes.[52]

Don't give blindly, because if you give blindly, you may end up with nothing left to give to yourself; you might end up with an empty pot.

---

51 D Bach, 2004. *The Automatic millionaire — A Powerful one step plan to live and finish rich*. London: Penguin Group p 175-176

52 D Bach, 2004. *The Automatic millionaire — A Powerful one step plan to live and finish rich*. London: Penguin Group p 177-180

The best gifts of them all, are those that are unexpected

Unexpected giving is beautiful. It speaks straight from the heart so give someone flowers today. Tell a person you love them just by getting them random gifts. Go ahead, surprise someone today and see how they feel, even a thank you card is enough to make someone's day.

When you give a present to someone unexpectedly, it speaks volumes about your character, and how much you value that person.

A friend told me a story his father once told him, about a man who walked for over an hour to get to the farm for work. He always prepared a packed lunch from home to eat at work. One morning, on his way to work, he bumped into a man begging for money. He told the man that he did not have any money but suggested that he could share his lunch with him.

He then carried on walking to work. He had arrived to work late at this particular time, which meant he would be at least half an hour late for his lunch. He went to sit on the stone he always sat on to have lunch.

Before he could sit down, one of the co-farmers came up to him and told him to look at a huge snake, that had been killed where he was about to sit. He was told that he was lucky to have come half an hour late because the snake was hanging around his stone earlier.

He was ever so thankful for having shared his lunch with that man because that act of giving saved his life.

Giving is a personal choice that should be planned for, and boundaries must be set. You must stay in control because once you are out of control, you will lose confidence and perhaps even shed a tear or two. It would help if you did not lose yourself in the novelty of giving; your wellbeing must have a balance in everything you do. You may sometimes have to say no to people and live with your boundaries. Saying no is not a bad thing, this is a sign of being a good manager, an amazing steward of God's money.

I have asked people for support, and they have said no to me, but I carried on regardless because no means that there is a new opportunity.

When the heart speaks to you, you have to listen. However, remember that you were also given the head for a reason: to think before you decide to spend your money and give it to others.

When you have decided to automate your money regarding what you have to save, you should also add how much money you can afford to give and if so, work towards that 10% for tithing.

Pick the charity, organisation or individual you would be giving to with diligence. Don't just take their word for it, do your research. Even if you are giving to the church, you must be diligent in your giving.

Here are a few things you should take into considerations before giving:

- How much can you realistically afford to give to this charity?

- Who are you giving the money to?
- Is there an alternative solution that is cheaper and efficient?
- Does this individual have a history of asking for money?
- How can you give in a way that is beneficial in the future for that person so that they do not have to ask for money again?
- What will the money be used for and is it for the right purpose?

Giving blindly is not a great idea because it might leave you unbalanced and would not encourage you to give again. It can lead you to resentment after you have given, which is not what giving is about.

An example of giving blindly is when you decide to give your money to a charity, only for you to get home and remember that you needed the money to buy a new cooker.

You want to be in a position to say: *"I gave to this charity. I really hope that the money can help them to achieve their goals. Thank God I had the means to help them as well as the means to support myself."*

Giving back to you

When was the last time you gave back to yourself? Gave yourself a present, a thank you gift or just showed yourself how much you love yourself?

You know you have worked hard for your money and have invested the time and energy to manage your finances;

you have shared your talents. How about loving you and giving back to the vessel that is building this empire?

You need to love and protect you and say yes to the things you want. The only way you can appreciate life, is when you learn to appreciate yourself and give yourself want you need and deserve.

Below are several ways you can give back to yourself:

Daily giving

» Daily exercising
» Drinking plenty of water throughout the day
» Getting the rest you need to function
» Eating the right foods
» Taking yourself on holiday
» Listening and reading about topics that will help you grow
» Having a moment of peace and being grateful for your amazing life
» Spending time with positive people that inspire you
» Spending time with family and building your bond

Quarterly giving

» Taking time out for yourself
» Going on weekend breaks without your family or friends
» Buying yourself an extravagant gift because you deserve it

Annual giving

> » MOT - yes, going and giving your body an MOT by going to your doctor, dentist, opticians and checking that you're physically and mentally well
> » Taking that luxury holiday or retreat away might mean delegating your work to someone else. How about flying first class because you can afford it?
> » Enjoying life and reminding yourself that life is good and the world is a beautiful place to live

Do whatever makes you happy, I may love reading for time out, but you may prefer going for a swim.

When the giver is not sincere

Giving on one hand and then taking it away by being verbally or physically mistreating someone, is an abuse OF POWER and not love. You may experience moments in your life when a person or community that gave you support, and end up verbally or physically abusing you or tormenting you directly, indirectly, or passively.

The abuse could be so bad and mentally testing that it wears out the giver's generosity. In toxic environments, you can start to have conflicting views. Although your mind may be grateful on one hand for the support you received, on the other hand, you could be thinking of an escape plan.

The same hand that is feeding you, could be the one that is destroying you spiritually. Some individuals could take years or decades to get out of that situation. If you do not feel 100% happy despite what you have been given, be assured that you know that the giver was never sincere in first place.

What happens when you give?

When you give to someone, you can change a person's future for the better. When you give, you can determine whether a person lives or dies. You can make history, mend a heart, or help cure a disease.

When you give, you can make someone smile and allow them to start seeing the possibilities of life. When you give, you empower, renew confidence, and allow that person to live in abundance.

I recall a time when City Gates Church, decided to pay half of the money for a trip for my daughter. Even after I said that I am getting a bonus from work which I can use to pay for the trip in full, they insisted. I was so overwhelmed with their generosity; I did not know what to do with it. I could not stop crying that Sunday because I felt nothing but pure love.

Do you recall a time when someone gave you support, whether it be financial support or just good advice or practical support?

How did it make you feel?

What results did you get from that support?

CHAPTER 7

Empower Financial Literacy for Your Children

> *" I believe the children are our future, teach them well and let them lead the way...*[53] *"*

How do you start teaching children about money? You can start teaching your children how to manage money by having honest and open conversations. Tell them what you know to be true (through your own experiences); the fortunes and misfortunes that you have had and why.

How you approach the conversation depends on your child's age. The older the child gets, the harder it becomes for them to listen to you because they are influenced by outside forces, which makes the conversation difficult.

I have two daughters, one who is 20 and one who is 7. With my 7-year-old, I teach her about money through storytelling. However, with the 20-year-old, I ask her

---

53 Songwriters: Linda Creed / Michael Masser, 1977, The Greatest Love of All; USA, lyrics © Sony / ATV Music Publishing LLC

to review my written material, leading us to have brief conversations about her thoughts.

In one of his sermons, Dr Myles Munroe stated that he paid his children money to read books about finances. He understood that while it may cost him $50 to get his children to read the books, it would save him thousands in the future.

Over the years, I have tried to play money-related games with my children during the holidays. The 20-year-old likes monopoly and she understands how it relates to life. Whereas, the 7-year-old understands a few things, but not enough to relate it to real life situations.

You can also use storytelling to teach your child financial literacy.

You could use a classic fairy tale and interpret the story in a different way to teach your children about money.

For example, in the *Three Little Pigs*, we learn that you must build your house with bricks and mortar so that the big bad wolf can't blow it down.

Here, you are teaching the child about materials and how good quality material is always better than poor quality. It saves you money and it can provide you with long-lasting protection from bad wolves. A bad wolf can be the wind or fire that might damage your house, if it's not built well.

Why not put a spin on the old classic tales and say something like:

"Once upon a time, there were three little pigs. Each of them worked hard and got paid three coins. One saved one

coin each time in the bank, which paid them more coins after (we call this interest).

The other one hid their one coin in the garden, but it never grew. The third pig's money became smaller as time went by because he spent it all and never put any coins aside for bad days.

When the pigs got older and sick, the pig that saved his money in the bank had even more money and could buy things with it. As he had so much money, he shared a little bit of it so that the other pigs could still eat and have medicine because sharing is caring. Which pig would you like to be?"

My 7-year-old said that she would like to be the pig that put money in the bank and earned interest and shared it with the others.

Another story can be about *Sleeping Beauty*. Instead of sleeping for thousands of years, she worked on a farm for thousands of years. Or she made chocolate bars and sold them for £3 to other people in the village.

She did three things with her three coins that she received:

1. She saved one of the coins in the bank, which paid her interest so that she could earn more money.
2. She spent one coin on food and bills.
3. She gave the third coin to help those who were unable to work because they were too ill or too old.

She then carried on working and thinking of more things to sell. She also thought about the services she could provide to others, by looking at her problems in the community.

In return, the people in the community gave her money for her time and effort. She continued to divide her money three ways, until one day, she found her prince working in the fields.

They worked hard together because they had dreams and goals. One day, they decided to put some of their money together to buy a home to live in, get married and have children.

The prince was so nice because he shared the bills, food, and other family expenses with Sleeping Beauty.

It would help if you retold the stories over and over again, like you do with children's fairy tales. Repeating the stories will help the children recall the information and perhaps also put it into practice.

You could then put what you have learnt into practice by getting three jars. Or for tighter security, three savings accounts regulated by the Financial Service Association (FSA) for your children. Every now and again, you could get them to divide their pocket money into those three accounts:

1. A Junior ISA that pays interest to save for future opportunities.
2. A savings accounts to save for new opportunities, just in case they can't earn any money.
3. Another savings account for spending money and giving

You could also allow your children to do chores around the house in exchange for money. Here, you are teaching them how to earn money.

It might be wiser to use clear jars at home because children can then see the money going in and how it's growing. Starting with a small amount of money and then seeing it grow in small increments can be encouraging.

I personally do not think you should pay children for cleaning their rooms. Cleaning their rooms is a chore that they should do as it will save them time and space. In return, they can use this to do other things and be able to find their belongings easily.

Under supervision, a small child should be allowed to see, touch and feel coins and paper money and be able to read the amount of money written on them.

Basic maths skills

You should teach your children the basic maths skills such as: addition; subtraction; multiplication; division; fractions and percentages. You should also explain how these concepts work in the real world with money.

BBC Bitesize teaches maths skills for different industries. For example, maths in hairdressing, etc.

Maths is not a subject that comes easy for some, however, once you start seeing how your money multiplies, how it can easily be divided and how percentages are used in everyday situations, you will become a better steward with it and be a better teacher for your children.

If you want to win this war on finances, you may have to go back to relearning basic maths. I went back to college to do my maths GCSE at the age of 30 - it empowered and liberated me.

The power in maths is not in the grade - the power is in the ability to count your change quickly. So that you know whether you are gaining or losing money.

Admittedly, teaching about money may not be easy in a cashless society because we use bank cards to pay for most purchases, but we can still try.

It's about the mindset

I was once at a seminar and a lady shouted out that the difference in how children from wealthy families in private schools are taught about money compared to children in state schools, is that the wealthy kids are taught that if they bought one house and proceeded to buy another house, they would have two houses.

Whilst state school children are taught one apple plus another apple is equivalent to two apples.

The wealthy kids in private schools are taught about assets and the children in state schools are taught about food. You need assets to leverage and get an income because they will always keep food on the table. Everything is down to the mindset and what you are exposed to.

How you behave

You have to be aware of your habits, address them, be open and realistic, share good practices and involve your children by asking them for their opinion. Communication is key to building wealth within the family.

Children like to mimic their parents

I remember when my older sister wanted to support a family member back in Uganda, the same way my parents had all these years. She had watched and seen my parents' kind nature and it inspired her to do the same thing.

She later found out that the relative lied about what he needed. For example, he would ask for triple the school fees; he tried to bleed her for every penny she had.

Had she discussed her intentions with my parents, they probably would have told her what to expect and how to best support those needing help.

The trouble with transparency

Sometimes sharing with your children means sharing your business with the whole world because children talk about being at home and what goes on at home to their peers and teachers.

At school, teachers ask children to write or talk about what they did on the weekends. So can you imagine, when a child goes to school and says that their mum has £300 in her account to spend on food this month, as part of their conversation with their teachers or peers. Nevertheless, lack of transparency can have a negative effect on how our children will manage their money in the future.

Who you allow to teach your children about finances is very important

I genuinely believe that the younger you are exposed to the realities of money, the better, but some lessons can be very brutal, damaging, and unfair on the innocent children. The truth of the matter is that despite your good intentions, someone is always out there to try and destroy your hard work.

Be careful who you allow to teach your children about money, because what the person teaches them could potentially damage their perception about how they deal with money and other things in life.

To illustrate my point further, I will tell you about a friend of mine - let's call her Bianca. Bianca once took her child to see her father. She joined him and his other children briefly and on that particular day, an old lady then came up to them and gave the children money for good behaviour.

As soon as the elderly lady left the room, the children's father asked the children for the coins. The children reluctantly did as they were told. He then said that any money they receive, must always be given to him.

Bianca was gobsmacked, she did not say anything to him because she honestly thought he was joking. As soon as she got home, she asked her son whether his father had given the money back to him and the child said he had he kept it. Bianca had no choice but to tell her son, never to give his father any money.

She could see that this man was about to start teaching his children to give him money and make them think that it was the norm at a very early age.

She also reflected on the fact that this was his behaviour throughout their entire relationship; he always borrowed money from her and never returned it.

Seek out those who have good habits

I have an Aunty who likes giving myself and my children treats. The one thing that I saw her do (which I think you should do), is examine all the receipts she gets and takes her time reading her receipts after each purchase. She ensures that all the items on the receipts have the right price, before leaving a shop or restaurant.

Some of us, grab the receipts and walk away really quickly making assumptions that the receipt and change are correct.

You should have people like her around your children. People who can teach you and your children to take note of every transaction you make, allowing no room for any mistakes.

Online purchasing

Teaching your children how to be mindful and not becoming addicted to buying items, especially online, is vital for developing healthy spending habits.

My 20-year-old has a habit of purchasing all goods online, particularly during the pandemic period which was almost two years. To be honest, most of us bought our goods online during this period and still do, but I never once thought of it as an addiction until my mother pointed it out.

I took a step back and analysed our thought processes and the actions we were taking every time we made a purchase online. I concluded that human beings love opening presents and getting nice things - it makes us feel loved.

Online shopping gives us the same feeling of receiving presents and being loved. The boxes are even more exciting when they are full of paper or sugar paper. The thought of searching for that item in the box feels us with excitement and raises our endorphins (the happy hormone). You get excited and look forward to opening those boxes. The more paper they have inside, the more your anticipation grows.

It's a feel-good factor that only lasts for a few hours or for that day. Because you love how it feels, you continue the habit repeatedly so that you get that feeling of excitement over and over again.

The only problem with this type of gifting is that you have spent your own money and not someone else's. Your money in your bank account would shrink little by little, until you have no money left in the account and by then it's too late.

I believe that we should all be mindful of online shopping and teach our children to do the same. Automating our money and creating an empowerment system should help limit this spending habit.

The spoken word

You teach your children about money with your actions and spoken words. If you speak with positivity and abundances, they will also speak with positivity and abundance. If you feel that your knowledge about finance is limited, start the journey of financial literacy with your children. This will only empower you and your family.

How about creating a financial game plan?

A financial game plan can be easily created for your child from the day you give birth. With all the information you now have or are accumulating, you should be able to create the financial game plan for each child and go through it each quarter. You can choose to adjust to it accordingly and you can choose whether you want to involve your children in the planning.

In summary, you should consider helping your children now and in the future by:

1. Sharing and telling them about money and how prosperity is created.
2. Creating a financial game plan which involves your children.
3. Continue building on your financial literacy whilst sharing your knowledge daily.

CHAPTER 8

Empower in Building a Lasting Legacy

" *The future beyond yourself
depends on you* "

Protect your wealth

It is in your best interest to protect your assets, businesses and yourself by getting the right insurance. The lie you may tell yourself is that you do not need insurance.

Being wealthy or mega rich means you will become a target. Every Tom, Dick and Harry will want to sue you if you happen to make a mistake or do something wrong (even if it's an accident).

You need car insurance

When I bought my first car, I could not afford the insurance and a friend advised me to get third party insurance until my finances were sorted out. He then proceeded to tell me not to drive too close to other cars. I have followed this rule, even when my finances improved, as I would prefer not to use my insurance.

People will try it, like a guy who took a video of me while opening my car door to see if I would touch his car. He intended to capture me on camera and then make a claim using the video as evidence. Luckily, I was aware of him and how much space I had between my car and his, so I took my time and entered the driver's seat. I also tell my children to be careful when they open car doors so they don't touch anyone's car. People are looking for money at every opportunity.

You need life insurance (especially if you have children)

A good friend of mine told me that when his mother died, he found out that she had taken out life insurance and as a result of that, his family gained financially. This encouraged him to take out life insurance so that his children would benefit from it.

You may need landlord insurance, building insurance, term time insurance or sickness protection

When you become a landlord, you will need landlord insurance and building insurance. Some people also get term time or critical illness insurance. Others may need sickness protection such as those who are entrepreneurs in case they fall ill and are not able to work.

Insurance costs vary, so it is important to compare at least three to four different quotes before taking out insurance. Read the small print to ensure that you know what you are getting yourself into. Go to the Money Saving Expert website to learn more about the different types of insurance (if you live in the UK).

When you protect yourself, you become more at ease if things go wrong, allowing you to relax and get on with your life. Insurance is not an emergency fund and it's not a quick 'get rich scheme' either. Insurance is a cover and umbrella that protects your wealth.

Cash is king

You should prepare for hard times by saving some cash because one person's loss may be your gain. For example, when you have spare cash available to you, you can buy goods and assets at a very low price. In a downturn, shares and stocks can become cheaper to purchase. You can even find cheaper house prices because a crisis can force some people to sell quickly to gain cash.

Insurance policies do not cover everything; therefore, you need to have some cash saved up. Some insurance companies may ask you to pay excess before they pay out.

Ensure you have some cash ready to use; cash is and always has been king. To further demonstrate this, I once heard an interviewer asking Warren Buffet why he kept so much cash as a reserve as part of his investment. He responded by saying that he kept cash reserves to protect his assets. Just in case someone tried to sue him for something, he wanted to be prepared.

'We don't prepare our children for life. We prepare our children for death' [54]

When you have built a legacy and created a foundation for your finances, you also must pass on your knowledge to the next generation so that the family legacy lives on.

Some of us believe that we are going to live forever. This is a lie from the pits of hell because we will all pass away some day

The best thing you can do is control what should happen to your assets and how they should be distributed when you pass away. You should also try and plan your funeral and how you want to be remembered. Preparing before you die is wise and makes the transition easier for your loved ones. They can grieve peacefully without worrying about finances.

It also stops people from bickering over who gets what. In your preparation, consider doing the following things.

- Write a Will to let everyone know how your assets should be distributed.
- Get a Power of Attorney, someone who will look after your financial affairs if you are not in the right frame of mind to do so.
- Put a Will in trust (if there are dependent children).

---

54 Father Dan, 2014, St Margaret & All Saints' Church

- Have your paperwork in order and passwords for your phones and emails, so that your loved ones can easily access information they might need.

A Will lets people know how you want your assets distributed and to whom. It has to be a valid Will, signed and witnessed by those who are not beneficials.

UK citizens can go to the Citizen Advice Bureau to get the following information about:

- Deaths and Wills
- What to do after a death
- Dealing with the financial affairs of someone who has died
- Arranging a funeral
- Complaining about a funeral
- Who can inherit if there is no Will (the rules of intestacy)
- What to do if someone dies abroad

Wills can be changed whenever your circumstances change. For example, if you get a divorce or have a change of heart about someone or things, you are free to change your Will any time. A Will can be contested in court; this is why you must be in your right state of mind when you write one.

In case of deterioration due to memory loss or dementia, appoint a trusted person with a written Power of Attorney. The person you nominate will be in charge of your estate and responsible for paying your bills.

A Trust

There are many different types of Trusts available in England and Wales and they can be used for different purposes. The main reason to use a Trust is to protect and manage financial assets. These assets could be money, land, property or investments. A property in Trust does not have to go through probate.

Types of Trusts:

Will Trusts (Also known as property trust)

If a couple own a property, they should consider whether to sign for the property as Tenants in Common or Joint Tenancies. A Tenancy in Common agreement allows only the percentage that the partner has contributed to be inherited by the children or whom they wish in their Will. This allows the other tenant in common to distribute or use their share as they wish. A Tenancy in Common suits cohabiting couples and blended families as it prevents complications of who gets what if there is a disagreement. However, a Joint Tenancy means that when one person dies, the other surviving spouse gets the entire property.

Discretionary Trusts

Trustees named in a Trust are responsible for distributing the income and assets for the benefits of the beneficiaries. A beneficiary may either be too young or unable to make certain decisions. A Trustee is trusted to make the right decisions regarding who will receive payment, if any salary or capital should be paid out when payments are made, and also be aware of any rules or regulations made on the beneficiaries.

Trustees will also help to carry out the estate according to the wishes of the person who has died.

Bare Trusts

A Bare Trust is a trust with a trustee who has no responsibilities or powers. A Bare Trust is usually done to support the young person receiving any income or capital gained from the estate.

For a list of different types of Trusts, please visit *gov.uk*.

Probate

If you would like to claim the property of your loved one after many years of not knowing that they had those assets, you would have to make a probate application. All forms and how to apply can be found at *gov.uk* for UK citizens. A probate can be applied for whether there is a Will or not. If a property is not claimed, it becomes the ownership of the Crown. These are some of the issues that can occur if you do not create valid Will.

When you die, it may take your relatives months and years (plus unexpected fees) to get a hold of your legacy and any property you have left behind for them.

It is important to get all your papers in order, to make life easy for your loved ones to find the paperwork and obtain the wealth you have worked hard for.

I have read several stories from newspapers about relatives not having a Will or the correct paperwork and as a result of this, not all the assets could be discovered. It also ended up costing their families even more money because some probate solicitors or firms took advantage of a person's lack of knowledge and sensitivity.

You can find the correct documents to complete and how much they cost on *gov.uk*

Taxes

Tax planning is essential because it helps you know how much you have to pay and how you can legally reduce your tax payments.

If you're running a business, your efforts should focus on how to maximise your income. Every penny you can save, counts towards your business and helps to run it.

I know many people who have been caught up in the world because they failed to pay their taxes and have been hit with a hefty tax fine. The fine occurred because they lacked financial literacy in that area.

I knew a man, let's call him John, who was a great salesperson. He was absolutely brilliant at selling face to face. He knew how to market himself and sell, sell, sell. What he failed to do was to pay his taxes. He knew how to make the money, and his bank account was bouncing.

I saw him make the money and it blew my mind at how easily people would buy goods from him. He knew both the products and his clients.

Not too long ago, John rang me up and told me he was fined over £25,000 for not paying his taxes.

Instead of him working out a payment plan with HMRC, continuing his business, and learning from his mistakes, he started to think that this was God's way of telling him that he had sinned and was cursed. It was clearly not a curse, he had a pretty good business, but he was so shocked by the fine that he gave up on building his business. He went and got himself a 9-5 job instead, which paid him half of what he was previously earning.

I am not a tax expert or licence tax advisor, but I have learnt a few things which I think can help you get your foundations right. Things that I wish I knew before getting into business.

1. As an employee, find out how much tax you have to pay and what your tax code is. You may have an incorrect tax code (this is often an emergency tax code) - the money will be reimbursed once you inform HMRC.

2. If you are self-employed in the UK, get your UTR number and an accountant. Keep all the receipts from everything you have bought for your business from day one. Create a folder and keep moving the receipts into that folder, take photos of paper receipts and upload them to that folder. Your accountant will need all of these documents. There are apps that can also help you with your tax accounts.

3. If you are self-employed, how much tax you pay depends on your income, minus expenses and

allowances. You should look up the tax allowance for each earning bracket. This number is subject to change. Then get the tax bracket and minus it from your income. The balance should give you an overall idea of how much tax you should be paying per month or yearly.

Deduct this amount from your earnings into a separate account or pay it ahead of time to HMRC. If you have overpaid, you will get the cash reimbursed back to you (which feels nice). The idea here is to ensure that there are no surprises at the end of the tax year. It's bad enough that you may have overspent for Christmas, but imagine getting your household bills along with an unexpected tax bill.

4. Talk to a tax planner or your accountant about how you can reduce the bill (if rules allow it). Remember the more money you have, the more you can give to charities of your choice.
5. Set aside money to pay your accountant and tax planner.
6. Check all your paperwork before signing on the dotted line. Everything your accountant does impacts your business; the taxman will come after you if the accountant makes a mistake.

Here is a list of different taxes according to the business entity in the UK:

1. Corporation tax - tax on corporations
2. Income tax – tax on individuals

3. Capital gains tax - sales on investments
4. Tax on dividends - if you're a share holder of a company
5. Gift tax - imposed on the person giving the gift (if the person has not died after seven years, there is no tax to be paid)
6. Inheritance tax - money paid from the deceased estate
7. Negative income tax (if you receive state benefits, this is applied as taxable income)
8. Value-added tax - on goods and services above a certain threshold
9. National insurance - in order to work in the UK you must have NI number.

To learn more about UK taxes, please visit *gov.uk* and talk to your accountant or tax planner.

I really believe that from the moment you are born, a tax bill is indirectly leveraged on the goods your parents or carers buy for you. You then pay taxes throughout your lifetime.

The lie you might tell yourself is that the less you earn, the less tax you will pay.

I knew a guy called Derek who was in debt. He told me that he would not get another source of income because he will get taxed more.

When he saw how I coached my clients to find other sources of income and how they got results, he took my advice and got himself another job. In return, he had more disposable income which he could use to both pay off his debt and entertain the ladies.

Some folks are even afraid to work overtime for the same reason. The last time I worked overtime, the extra cash paid for the painters, YouTube equipment and my regular bills. Yes, I was taxed, but that was the least of my worries.

My motto is to work and get paid the money you deserve. You must also pay your taxes accordingly because no matter what, it is a win-win to earn more money.

Do not attach yourself to money. You came into this world empty-handed and will transit out of the world in the same way. You cannot take the money with you. I suggest that you do what you need to do whilst following the rules. Money will come in abundance if you allow it to.

CHAPTER 9

Empower in Affirmations

You need encouragement from time to time to keep you motivated and enthused whilst on this financial empowerment journey.

Affirmations are powerful words in a sentence that can motivate you, encourage you and elevate you to the next level of achievement. The right words should be able to move you into action so that you can fulfil your full potential in life whilst creating a fulfilled legacy.

I encourage you to create your own affirmations as well as use affirmations from other sources. This will help you: earn more; spend wisely, overcome doubts; save and invest.

Here are some of the affirmations that you can use daily to help you stay on the journey to a fulfilled legacy.

Empower in earning

If you are experiencing rejection, this affirmation should remind you of the potential you have to earn more money.

Affirm by speaking out loud: *"I am amazing!"* Repeat this affirmation five times.

You will slowly start to smile because you will realise once again that you are an absolutely amazing human being, with the potential to do more and be more.

Empower in spending affirm

When you are about to make a huge purchase and you're feeling overwhelmed or uncertain about it, pray about it first.

Affirm by saying repeatedly before making the decision that *"This is God's money and I must manage it well."*

It is important to ask yourself this question: *"Am I being a good manager with God's money?"* If you do not believe in God, you can still use this affirmation by asking yourself a question, 'am I managing this money well"?

Empower in overcoming money blocks

It is inevitable that from time to time, you will make the wrong decisions or judgements that may have a negative financial impact on you or others around you.

If you end up making the wrong decision, remember that you are human and we all make mistakes.

Affirm by quoting: *"Money works in my favour"* and repeat this when you're feeling anxious about that mistake. This should remind you that each mistake is a lesson and the wins are blessings. Forgive yourself and learn new ways of doing things better. Always work on improving yourself and teaching others when given the opportunity.

Empower in savings

When you are struggling to save, remind yourself of the following:

> 66 *Cash is king - without it, my options are limited therefore I must save.*

Remember that even the rich have limits on their spending, so why not you?

Empower in investments

Achieving financial independence is when money works for you, not the other way around.

Affirm: *"Money works for me; I don't work for my money!"* Repeat this daily and this should help you continue to invest, or to prepare to invest the money you're saving.

In the Bible, the one who multiplied his talents and returned God's money received more money. God will give you more if you do well with the little you have, as long as you put His money to good use.

Empower in giving

Remember that your purpose in life is to serve others with your gifts. Don't hold back your talents; show them off to the world and give all that you can.

Affirm: *"I am here for a purpose!"* Repeat this daily - this affirmation should help you step into your purpose and encourage you to give your services to others with love.

Affirm the truth

When your finances are not yet where you would like them to be, affirm by using these words I heard from Les Brown:

> 66 *I have a temporary cash-flow problem.*

A positive attitude will move you to the right direction and enable you to make money moves that will improve both your finances and wellbeing. Remember to chase purpose and not money.

To conclude

If you do nothing at all, please search for wisdom and understanding to gain clarity when it comes to creating wealth. In return, this will help you make the right decisions.

As always, I wish you tremendous wealth and a healthy lifestyle.

For support to fulfil your full potential in life, I urge you to visit *sandrakaima.com* so that you can live the life that you deserve for yourself and your family.

Resources

sandrakaima.com

patricewashington.com

thehumblepenny.com

Super Simple Investment. *https://sky08--financialjoyacademy.thrivecart.com/super-simple-investing/*

Munroe, Dr. Myles, (2003) The Principles and Power of Vision; Keys to achieving Personal and Corporate Destiny, Witticker House, Nassu, Bahamas

Munroe, Dr. Myles (1991) Understanding Your Potential: Discovering the Hidden You, Destiny Image publishers Inc. Shippensburg, PA

Munroe, Dr. Myles 2018. Understanding The Purpose And Power Of Women: God's Design for Female Identity, Expanded Edition with study guide, Nassau, Bahamas United States: WHITAKER HOUSE

Munroe, Dr. Myles, (2002) Releasing your Potential - Exposing the Hidden You, Published in Partnership - Destiny Image and The Diplomat Press, Nassau, Bahamas

Bach, D., (2018) Smart Women Finish Rich- 8 Steps to achieving Financial Security and Funding Your Dreams. 2nd Edition. United States: Currency (CurrencyBooks.com) p 337

Bach, D.,2004. The Automatic millionaire—A Powerful one step plan to live and finish rich. London: Penguin Group

Influence marketing Hub, (2022) "How Many YouTube Views Do You Really Need to Make Money". [online] Available at: *influencermarketinghub.com/youtube-views-to-make-money*

Kaima, H., (2022) My Arrogant Friends - The Rise and Fall and Fall of Uganda. JoeNeDoe Company U.K

Lapin, Rabbi D. (2014) Business Secrets from the Bible: Spiritual Success Strategies for Financial Abundance, New Jersey/Canada: Wiley.

Kiyosaki, R T. (2017) Rich Dad Poor Dad, 3rd Edition – 20th Anniversary edition, United States of America: Plata Publisher. LLC

EG Siyaga, (2021) Dr. Myles Munroe On Chinese Secret For Dominion. *youtube.com/watch?v=inx-QBPjTpQ* (Uniform Resource Locator) [20/11/2022].

Amanda Smith, (2014). Oprah interviewing: Robert Kiyosaki: [YouTube], Available at: *facebook.com/watch/?v=345673923348135* (Accessed 10.01.2023)

Clason S. George. (2015) The Richest Man In Babylon. Original Edition. Milton Keynes: DAUPHIN PUBLICATIONS.

R Sethi, 2020. I Will Teach You To Be Rich. 2nd Edition. London: Yellow

Elizabeth Narins, 2015: How Your Cycle Makes You Spend Money in Weird Ways [online] Available at: *cosmopolitan.com/health-fitness/a39084/how-your-cycle-affects-your-shopping-habits* [Accessed 27 Nov 2022]

Melissa Leong, 2014: Why do we spend? What science says about our personal finances- Why do we spend? What, in our brains, leads us to take on bigger mortgages than we can afford? Leading scholars explain our money behaviour [online] Available at: *financialpost.com/personal-finance/why-do-we-spend-what-science-says-about-our-personal-finance*

Step Change Debt charity, 2022, Putting together a full and final settlement offer [online] Available at: *stepchange.org/debt-info/settlement-offers-to-creditors.aspx* [accessed 29th November 2022]

C, James, 2018. Atomic Habits –An Easy and Proven Way to Build Good Habits and Break Bad Ones: Tiny Changes, Remarkable Results - Penguin Random House, London

Dave Darby, 2020.What's wrong with billionaires? [online] Available: *lowimpact.org/posts/whats-wrong-with-billionaires* [Accessed 28 November 2022].

Devika Rao, 2022. Why do people hate billionaires? [online]Available: *theweek.com/economy/1018418/why-do-people-hate-billionaires* [accessed 28th Nov 2022]

Rachel Rodgers, 2022: We should all be millionaires [online] Available: *helloseven.co/the-book*

Lewis Howes; 2021: How I MAKE $27,000 / Week With Passive Income & Productivity Secrets | Ali Abdaal & Lewis Howes [online] Available: *youtube.com/watch?v=UJoZMuxx0T8&t=3271s* [accessed 28 November 2022]

TD Jakes. 2016; Grounded in Finance [online] Available at: *dailymotion.com/video/x5c9ad8* [accessed 28 November 2022]

Bank of England, 2021. What do I need to know about debt [online] Available at: *bankofengland.co.uk/knowledgebank/what-do-i-need-to-know-about-debt* (accessed 26th January 2023)

Founder, Martin Lewis. Editor - Chief, Marcus Herbert 2022 Cutting your costs, fighting your corner. [online] Available at: *moneysavingexpert.com*

www.moneysavingexpert.com Step Change Debt charity, 2022, Putting together a full and final settlement offer [online] Available at: *stepchange.org/debt-info/settlement-offers-to-creditors.aspx* [accessed 29th November 2022]

Catey Hill, 2018. Moneyish. [online] Available at: *marketwatch.com/story/this-common-behavior-is-the-no-1-predictor-of-whether-youll-get-divorces-2018-01-10* [Accessed 26 Nov 2022]

Wells Fargo, 2022. Comparing the snowball and the avalanche methods of paying down debt [online] Available at: *wellsfargo.com/goals-credit/smarter-credit/manage-your-debt/snowball-vs-avalanche-paydown/#:~:text=In%20contrast%2C%20the%20%22avalanche%2* [accessed 29th November]

D. Ramsey, 2003 The Total Money Makeover Work Book, Nashville, Tennessee: Thomas Nelson

Wikipedia, 2022, Parable of the talents or minas [website] Available: [accessed 5 December 2022] *en.wikipedia.org/wiki/Parable_of_the_talents_or_minas#:~:text=According%20to%20the%20abilities%20of,a%20significant%20amount%20of%20money*

Paul Lewis (@paullewismoney) / Twitter

You and Yours - BBC Radio 4

About The Author

Sandra Kaima is a Speaker, Author, and Empowerment coach. An advocate for financial independence, mental and physical health.

She conducts a financial empowerment program as well as being an advocate for wellbeing.

An inspiring single mother of two children. She has impacted on over thousands of individuals, to be empowered, have renewed confidence, and live in abundance with her coaching ability.

She is an award winner for Transformation and Innovation and has been nominated for Changing Futures from London and Home Counties.

She is a world class leader who is purpose driven and has a burning desire to support individuals succeed in life.

She believes that we all have the resources to fulfil our full potential in life and that nothing is impossible given the right tools and with good coaching we can all overcome the financial burden and manage our health in a way that makes sense to us to build a lasting legacy.

Her book. "A Fulfilled Legacy" "How to overcome money lies and have financial freedom" - is a definite game changer. This book will change legacies globally, it will elevate and inspire you to be more and do more for yourself and others connected to you. Are you ready to take action?